SMALL BUSINESS
EXIT LESSONS

Setting Up and Running Your Company
with the Exit Mindset for
Small Business Tech Entrepreneurs

Shahri Naghshineh

Printed in the United States of America

Published in Hellertown, PA

Cover and interior design by Leanne Coppola

Images by Jenny Giandomenico

Library of Congress Control Number 2023900241

ISBN 978-1-958711-29-3

For more information or to place bulk orders, contact the author or the publisher at Jennifer@BrightCommunications.net.

BrightCommunications.net

*To all those entrepreneurs and business owners with grit
who overcome adversity and crisis to reach their goals*

*To Inventors and Innovators in Science, Technology,
Engineering, Arts and Marketing:* **STEAM**

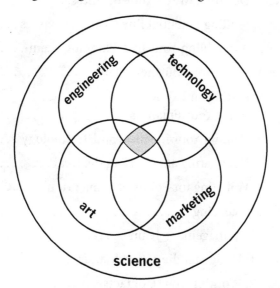

*To the team of Ben Franklin Technology Partners of
Northeastern Pennsylvania, who have been supportive of
most of my startups*

And to my father, Ali M. Naghshineh

Contents

Foreword

In my more than 30 years of professional services as a former CPA and now a practicing attorney, I have handled numerous business transactions. Not surprisingly, each transaction takes on its own persona.

Having had the pleasure of working with Shahri Naghshineh for more than 20 years, I've found he brings a unique, 360-degree perspective to business transactions because of his skills in both the scientific arena as well as business. Importantly, in his adventures, he also nurtured the human component of operating his businesses, discovering the importance of engaging human capital without sacrificing control.

As you will shortly discover, Shahri readily acknowledges his strengths and more importantly his weaknesses. He did his research, asked tough questions, attempted to outline where the pitfalls lie, acknowledged where he made his mistakes, and shared what characteristics helped him achieve his success. He reevaluates what has changed over the years as a result of the extremely competitive environment in which we now live—where there are no longer rules of professional business conduct! Sadly, it has become a grab-and-steal, competitive environment to achieve one's business aspirations.

This treatise is a commonsense, practical outline of the do's and don'ts of the many options to consider when embarking on a new business venture. Shahri invites you to explore and experience its many phases—some successful, others not—while maintaining a view toward the ultimate exit strategy.

Shahri has done a masterful job of guiding you through very complex decisions—without tangling you in the weeds. Enjoy! It's an adventure!

—Dolores Laputka, Esq., Norris McLaughlin Attorneys at Law, Allentown, PA, February 2023

Foreword

Whether you're just starting your entrepreneurial journey or feeling like you're nearing the end of it, the question of how to exit is never far from your mind. The road from on-ramp to off-ramp in the high-tech venture world is filled with navigational challenges, and you can think of this book by my friend Shahri Naghshineh, filled with candid lessons and valuable insights, as a critical component in your venture's GPS.

A question that my fellow investors often ask of founders making their initial pitch is, "What's your exit strategy?" Too often, the question comes when the company hasn't even developed their first product, brought on its first team member, or sold one dollar worth of product. The book you're about to read affirms my belief that asking a founder about how their company journey will end before the journey has even begun is an answerless question indeed. In fact, my experience over 25 years of seed-stage investing, like the stories that unfold on the following pages, proves again that the exit finds the company rather than the other way around.

While I certainly understand why potential investors ask the question, it always seems premature and borderline rude to ask it so early in the company journey. It is almost as if the investor is asking, "If I make an investment, how long do I have to be in this relationship with you?" The entrepreneurial journey is long and undulating. There are pivots and lawsuits and unpredictable external factors. There are mistakes, regulatory changes, and team members who need to be terminated. Shahri tells you about his experience with all of these and more. With all that can and will go wrong, how would anyone be able to predict likely future outcomes?

Despite all this, we do prepare our clients to answer the question "what is your exit strategy?" As my friend will herein point out, Ben Franklin Technology Partners of Northeastern Pennsylvania (BFTP-NEP) was a very early financial and strategic supporter of his ventures over three decades. BFTP-NEP is a state-funded organization that was created in 1982 to invest in, mentor, and incubate companies just like those that Shahri has created. I'm the Chief Investment Officer for the organization, which gives me a birds-eye view of a portfolio of 180 companies at any one time, and probably 500 since I joined the organization in 2000. We have more than $25 million invested in those companies, and we've seen companies go public, get acquired by large and small companies, continue to operate independently, and fail altogether.

Our experience tells us to coach the founders to be confident but evasive when answering the question about exit strategy during their investor meetings. The response I wish I could teach every founder to give, and that will help loosen investor purse strings, would go something like this:

> *"We'll exit through strategic buyout. But first, we plan to build a fast-growing and cash-flow positive business that fills a market niche that about a dozen Fortune 1000 acquisitive businesses do not currently address. When we've*

> *built that value and are of a size that is of inter-*
> *est to one of those companies, we'll explore our*
> *options to get the best value for our sharehold-*
> *ers in a competitive strategic buyout process.*
> *For now, though, we're just getting started and*
> *focused on daily execution."*

All of this is meant to demonstrate to the investor that you share her interest in one day selling the company to get everyone's investment back with a return. That is, you have a plan *to* exit—but make no mistake—as you'll see from Shahri's wisdom, there is no strategy for an exit other than good execution and a little luck.

My work at BFTP-NEP begins when companies are first brought into the world. Often, our founders have never launched a venture before the one they launch with us. A second-time founder who successfully exited a first venture certainly gets at least a small benefit of the doubt from investors on the second venture. Does that mean the second venture is easier? Not a chance. But investors know that a second-time founder has built up some anti-body resistance to the most damaging mistakes.

One of those mistakes Shahri avoided on venture #2 was taking on significant outside investor capital and sharing board control. Another was developing inter-nal manufacturing capacity. These decisions worked out great as he navigated venture #2 to another successful exit and avoided the many complications outside capital and capital intensive manufacturing can present.

But the truth is, it could just as easily gone badly and the personal wealth he earned from venture #1 could have vanished as he navigated his self-financed ship through the roiling seas and shallow shoals of outsourced man-ufacturing in venture #2. As Shahri demonstrates in this book, each venture is unique and takes a different path to success or failure.

A final memory I had while reading Shahri's book was of one of the many conversations we had in my office, or in the lobby, or in his lab. Early in my time at BFTP-NEP, there was a chance meeting in my office between Shahri and Fred Beste, a wonderful venture capitalist from our region. Fred was in my office when Shahri walked by, saw Fred, and stopped in. Fred had mentored Shahri early in his first venture. Now, several years into his second venture, Shahri came in beaming, and said, "Fred, we've had a great outcome with our business!" Fred, who had been sitting on the edge of the small conference table in my office, stood and heartily reached out to shake Shahri's hand saying, "Congratulations! How big was the exit!?"

As it turns out, Shahri's big news was not an exit, but rather a first big client. This moment taught me how differently founders and investors look at the meaning of success. And I think the biggest lesson from this book is that getting a thousand small things right is what it takes to get the final big thing right.

—Wayne K. Barz, Chief Investment Officer, Ben Franklin Technology Partners of Northeastern Pennsylvania, Bethlehem, PA, December 2022

Introduction

Are you considering selling your business or licensing your technology? STOP! Team up, take your time, and prepare. Ask yourself: Is this the right time to sell your business or license your technology? Is the potential buyer or licensee the right partner for you? When selling or licensing to a much larger company, the odds are not in your favor. Learn from the lessons in this book to improve your odds. Selling your business is like betting against the house when playing in a casino.

Let's make sure you do not regret the decision down the road, having walked away from millions of dollars, like many of us did. After we sold our second business, we left behind almost $27 million—and even more in potential earnings. We know it is not going to be a win-win deal, but what can you do to make a better deal? If the buyer and/or the licensee misrepresents the facts and does not perform intentionally, what options do you have?

In this book, you will learn why selling your business or licensing your technology is a marathon—not a sprint. It is time consuming. It is emotional. It is intense. It is a major distraction from focusing on growing your business. So, you need an exit plan and support. This book will give you the tools and show you how to use them.

Use this book to guide you to adopt your exit mindset, build and execute your exit plan, and max out on monetizing your exit. Let's get you to make a win-win deal.

In this book, we are focused on deals for small businesses with annual revenues up to approximately $50 million.

The successful small business owners with profitable, growing businesses will find this book's exit lessons to sell and/or license their businesses very useful.

If this is your first business, you can learn a lot from our experiences. You need to work smart, have fun, live well, make time for family and friends, continue self-fulfillment, and exit successfully. It does not matter what your background is. Many entrepreneurs come from humble backgrounds. Our parents worked hard to raise our family. Many struggled to make ends meet. Some of us, like me, are immigrants who have left behind mother countries to continue with their education.

Now it's time to prepare and use a plan to guide you through the exit stage. Let's call it your exit plan. Throughout this book, you'll learn what items you should include in your exit plan, and at the end of this book, in Appendix F, is an outline to use to create your plan. The plan is a map for navigating uncharted waters and developing the needed mindset. You need to get buy-in from your team as well as the interested third parties. So, we begin with a review of the essential parts of the plan to define the business and plan for the path ahead—and then the successful exit. You will find lessons and suggested actions to take to add value to your business throughout the business plan review.

Let's make sure you secure better exit deals than many other business owners I interviewed and I did. The lessons in this book should provide you with guidance for a smoother exit or licensing experience. You need to make sure you know the intrinsic worth of your company, technology, your business market potential, and yourself. This book's objective is to assist you to continue to grow your business profitably while you're involved in selling your business or licensing your technology.

How do I know? I have been called a self-made businessman and a serial entrepreneur. I am an immigrant, father, and an engineer. I am fortunate to have founded and cofounded five specialty chemical businesses, invested in five, sold two, licensed two, closed two. I have been blessed with outstanding mentors and consultants throughout my career. I could have retired three times so far. (But retirement is overrated.) I have been a business consultant to private equity investment firms, investigating potential acquisition of other small businesses. I have mentored the owners of more than five other technology-based companies, two of which have been very successful. But not all. And I would do it again.

I was the hands-on president of each of my businesses. Both of the businesses we sold within 5 years generated $100 million in annual sales for the new owners, so I learned. The profit margins are estimated to be significantly above 70 percent.

Most of the products we developed are still in use after 20 years in semiconductor fabrication production lines. These products continue to provide large revenue streams. We were paid only $14 million for the first business we sold, and we were paid only $22 million in total payouts for the second one. Also, there were poorly structured and compensated employment agreements. We had to endure full or partial loss of control over our businesses shortly after the deals were concluded. The same can be said about the licensing deals we made. Plus, there were unexpected changes imposed on the structure of the acquired businesses. We had limited recourse over these changes. We were not prepared because we did not have exit plans.

Even though the technology licensing deals we made worked well initially, they were terminated within a few years. We licensed three companies to produce and sell our products developed by the three different businesses we started. Licensing deals are easier to make than merger and acquisition deals, but they are more difficult to manage. Here again, we walked away from significant revenue based on royalties due.

Many former business owners tell of similar outcomes. But you might be asking, as smart as we think we are, how could we?!

Let this be a lesson: Plan, prepare, establish the exit mindset, and execute well on the exit plan before and after the deal is done.

Let's turn the deal from win (you)-WIN (the buyer) into WIN-WIN!

I've been making notes, attending seminars, and collecting articles for writing a book on entrepreneurship since 1995. That was soon after we sold our first business. While conducting my research for this book, I interviewed eight other former business owners who have sold their businesses. Many had similar personal experiences. Almost all who sold their first business found the process taxing and the outcome less than satisfactory. Most of us think we could have done much better.

Over the years, you have put your time, blood, sweat, tears, and focus into your business. You had to be persistent to grow a profitable venture—despite the obstacles, minefields of poor advice, sometimes not-so-great decisions, and no's. You recovered from crises, pivoted, and learned from your mistakes. You kept going. You have grit, drive, agility, and vision. You made sacrifices—such as not spending time with your family—to bring your vision to life. And now you have decided it's time to move on.

And now, maybe you have been approached with offers to buy your business and/or license your technology. Perhaps your customers and/or potential customers have suggested you sell the business or license your technology to a larger supplier of theirs. You might want to monetize your efforts. Or you are considering cashing out options. You may want to retire. Or the co-owners want out. It's time.

Included in this book are important lessons for planning your exit, such as not to settle for the first offer. Let the market decide what your business is worth. Do not settle for what you will be happy with when the buyer might be willing to pay much more for your business. Do not leave a lot of money on the table. What if your business is worth 10X more to the buyer than what you are willing to settle for? You owe it to yourself and to your co-owners, staff, and all those who have supported your business. In fact, the buyer will respect you more and feel better about the deal if you negotiate well. Negotiating for a better offer also minimizes buyer's remorse. The buyer must not feel he overpaid for the deal. That leaves a bad taste, which impacts future interactions.

Let's shine a light on the path of a growing successful business and ease the owner's exit journey experience. (However, it is not possible to provide in one book all the paths you can take to ensure your successful exit.) Hence we are setting up www.ExitLessons.com, where we plan to continue investigating the options to exit a business. In this book, I review the business stock purchase acquisition option and technology licensing deals—rather than asset purchase or any other exit options.

I sincerely wish for you to accomplish your exit goals, including continuing to live your American Dream. You deserve a successful exit. So, get prepared.

Contact me at www.ExitLessons.com.

CHAPTER 1
Deciding to Sell Your Business

Why do you want to sell your venture? Has a buyer made you an offer you cannot refuse? My advice is to be very careful! And move forward cautiously. Take your time.

Looking back, what intrigues me about the businesses we sold is wondering: *Why do people often agree to terms that we do not fully understand when a buyer dangles money in front of us?* I have found that this is a common feeling among business owners who have sold their businesses.

Here are some reasons my friends and I, all entrepreneurs and business owners, who have been through acquisitions and licensing deals have experienced.

- It is time to monetize our success: to enjoy the fruits of our labor after all these years.

- We want to retire. It's time to sell the business and start the next phase of our lives.

- We need the recognition that comes with being a successful entrepreneur.

- We want to validate our success by having a third-party company buy our venture.

- To reach the next level of expansion, we need to team up with another firm.

- The cofounders can no longer work together.

- The investors want to cash out.

- Customers recommended or requested the sale to ensure their supply source reliability.
- A buyer has made you an offer that you cannot refuse.
- More often than we care to admit: The business has been bought to save it and the owners from burnout, implosion, and collapse.

If a potential buyer has approached you, why do they want to buy your business? Here are some possible reasons.

- They want to enter a high growth niche fragmented market
- Have your talented team members
- Penetrate strategic accounts
- Access strategic territories
- Acquire technology that has multiple potential applications for their different divisions
- Potential for reducing overhead by consolidating back-room operations and production
- Multiple applications of your core technology by their various divisions
- Owner/operator who can be readily replaced given the depth of the business talent
- Get revenge, get even with a competitor of your firm
- Prevent competitors from buying your firm
- Improve margins and grow sales
- Keep up with rapid changes in customer product/service needs
- Buy and shelve your technology, which they perceive as a threat

- Reduce their investment or augment their internal R&D resources
- Capitalize on your impressive patent portfolio

Usually, a combination of the above reasons motivates the buyers.

Unfortunately, far too often the buyers dramatically make out better in the acquisition than the sellers. Here are some reasons why.

- We jump at the first offer to buy our business.
- We are impatient because most of us have ADHD.
- We are too busy running our own business.
- We trust the buyer's intentions at our own peril.
- We do not understand the terms and conditions.
- The cofounders can no longer work together.
- We underestimate the impact of our business.
- We underestimate the Not Invented Here (NIH) syndrome at the buyer's organization.
- Our venture is running out of funds.
- This is our first deal, and we do not understand how Mergers and Acquisitions (M&A) are conducted.
- We cannot cope with the culture shock.
- We did not include clawback clauses.

Usually, the buyer's experienced M&A team negotiates from a position of strength, playing the reluctant buyer. They have dedicated M&A staff who are experienced in pulling off a win (you)-WIN (buyer) deal for the buyer organization. Their staff are all over your business, asking questions and interviewing your team. They do a good job with the SWOT analysis (strengths, weaknesses, opportunities, and threats—more on this on page 82). Make sure everyone on your management team is on board with your decision to exit. Keeping all co-owners in line is the most difficult and stressful part of the exit plan.

CHAPTER 2
Finding Potential Buyers and Licensees

How can you find potential buyers? There are four typical ways.

Potential Buyers Find You

In both businesses we sold, we were approached by a potential buyer. I consider them to have been *strategic* buyers. These were both publicly traded companies that were also active in our semiconductor fabrication growing market niche. They were not direct competitors. They wanted to expand their product line offerings to the same customers. They also were very interested in our accounts in Asia. We hired a business broker in our industry to manage the opportunity to sell our business. Also, the licensees of my third and fourth businesses products and technology approached us.

You Find Potential Buyers

If you are trying to find potential buyers, look for synergy. You already have many contacts in your industry. In many cases, your service/product is used with or in combination with other products. The suppliers of those synergistic products would make good potential buyers for your business. Also, look for other businesses that want to move into your market. Private equity firms are also buying businesses. I have met with the management teams of two of these firms. They have purchased multiple businesses in the chemical industry market. They buy several small businesses, then bundle them and resell them as one entity. Even if you identify potential buyers, let your exit plan advisor screen and qualify them for you. (More on exit plan advisors on page 22.)

For our fifth business, we pursued licensing our technology to a few competitors. We were unsuccessful. But our competitors learned a lot about our technology. It was a huge mistake of ours.

A Business Broker Finds Potential Buyers

Another way to find potential buyers is with a broker. Find a broker who is familiar with your industry, as we did for both of the businesses we sold. Each time after we were approached by a potential buyer, we hired the broker to shop the business. We wanted to receive multiple bids so that we could better determine the value of our business. The broker reached out to his own contacts in the industry, and he brought more potential buyers to the table. A broker might also be able to dig up industry multiples used for calculating the value of your business. Our broker was also aware of other similar businesses that were acquired. (More on business brokers on page 24.)

Customers Suggest Potential Buyers

In a few cases, our customers suggested other companies we should team up with. In two separate cases, interested potential customers told us they would use our product if we had a dominant competitor license our technology. In a third case, a potential customer suggested that if we were bought out by a larger firm—one of their existing qualified suppliers—they would purchase our product. In these cases, supply source reliability was the driving force. We attempted to negotiate licensing tools, but soon after we walked away from making deals with our competitors.

For more details on various aspects of the M&A processes of large businesses, I recommend the book *Selling Your*

Startup by Alejandro Cremades. Alejandro's book is especially useful for M&A deals worth more than $100 million.

Selling or Licensing to Your Competitor

You might have noticed I said there were four options to finding potential buyers, and this is the fifth listed. That's because I don't recommend this one. Most of the time, this option does not work. Avoid including competitors in the bidding process to buy your business or license your technology. I think the outcome is not going to be to your satisfaction, and it can often be to your detriment.

When selling your business, if one of your competitors shows interest, make sure they are committed to bid. Make sure they are not only interested in gathering information—fishing for info. Be bold, ask them for an upfront, non-refundable, significant fee to get the bid package (prospectus). If they refuse to pay the fee, walk away. Let them know other companies are willing to put up money upfront—or at least let them think they are.

In both times, the same competitor participated, pretending to bid—only to back out last minute! They took all the tech and business info they could, and then they refused to bid. This very same competitor was successful in disrupting our third venture via alleged patent infringement.

DO NOT trust your competitors' motives! Also realize that exclusion is highly motivating to their management. In other words, by turning them down, they might become more interested and commit to paying the upfront fee.

While you are trying to attract buyers, hang in there and be calm and patient. It's like fishing: You have to put in the time and effort. You must be prepared and use the right fishing gear, bait, tackle, time, and location. Then be patient. If you build it, they will come.

Our Exit Plan Experience

In both startup companies we sold, we were approached by the potential buyers. We were not prepared. We did not have exit plans. So, we had to start working on our expedited exit plans with our lawyers, accountants, and a business broker we hired. The business broker identified and brought to the table a few more potential buyers. Interestingly, in each case only one buyer made an offer, negotiated, and purchased the venture. However, unfortunately three or more potential buyers, including one direct competitor, were provided with our business's prospectus.

Our first business was not sold to the first potential buyer that approached us. Our second business buyer's CEO, a publicly traded company, was motivated and had been tracking our business activities. The CEO was a former entrepreneur, too, and he and I connected and stayed friends even after my departure from his business. A few years later, they sold their business, too, and he semi-retired. In two of our licensing deals, we were also approached by the licensees.

I believe, given the continued success of the acquired businesses, we undervalued our ventures when we sold. However, in my first venture there was a serious fallout among the partners. We were fortunate to be able to sell the business before the business imploded.

The second venture, which was based on lessons learned and contacts made in the first business, was a successful startup with a good operating business plan. Even so, we could have negotiated a better deal when we sold it. After the deal was done and long after the earn-out period was completed, I noticed the earn-out formula was unrealistic. I should have never agreed to it. But I had not actually evaluated the earn-out formula before closing and during the earn-out period. The earn-out structure was set up in a way we could not reach the milestones in revenue. Fight for realistic earn-out milestones, and make sure you have sufficient control over the outcome.

In one incident, I found out the buyer's organization was planning to use our product position at one key account as a loss leader to sell their other products. They wanted us to agree to discount our product price to convince the customer to purchase other products from them. We agreed finally—under one condition: The buyer had to compensate us for the discount.

In retrospect, I should have spent more time understanding and negotiating the deals. We should have waited two or more years before selling the business. In the first deal, the pressures placed on us to conclude it due to internal almost fatal disagreements among the cofounders was the primary reason. In the second deal, I could have held out better, but I was stressed from managing a fast-growing business, and I was also dealing with personal issues at home. (A divorce can wreak havoc on one's motivation and business focus.)

Chapter 3
Assembling Your Exit-Planning Team

Even though you might have created your business all by
yourself, and then you might have run and grown it nearly
single-handedly, you can't exit it alone. You need several
key experts to support you. Here are some key members of
your successful exit team.

Exit Plan Advisor

Developing an exit plan is time-consuming, complicated, and at times quite emotional. The plan is best
developed and supported by an outside business advisor.
Preferably the advisor should be a businessperson with
significant experience in starting, growing, and selling or
licensing their own small businesses or technologies. You
need to trust the advisor. The advisor/consultant must be
able to relate to and have empathy for the owner/owners.

The exit plan advisor is *not* your lawyer nor accountant.
The exit plan advisor will manage the development and execution of the exit plan. The advisor will assist with the negotiations of the business sale. They are compensated with an
hourly fee and/or compensation calculated as a percent of
the purchase price. The exit plan advisor's service should
allow you to continue to manage and grow the business,
making it ready for sale at its highest intrinsic value.

In my two business sales, we did not have an exit plan
advisor, which might partially explain why we did not negotiate a better deal. That was a void that our business broker,
lawyers, and accountants could only partially fill. The exit

plan advisor will support the set up and execution of the exit plan and mindset. He/she will support the negotiations and advise on the details of the deal terms and conditions.

As I mentioned, for the sale of our first business our business broker was the closest thing we had to an exit plan advisor. He did an admirable job of walking us through the exit. He managed to save the first business from implosion prior to its acquisition. He did a good job hiding the owners' internal conflicts from the buyer. We used the same broker for both business acquisitions.

In retrospect, I should have also had an exit plan advisor for the sale of my second business. Fortunately, our broker, lawyers, and accountants did well delivering on their services.

Personal Financial Planner

You need to hire a personal financial planner to review and advise you on your personal finances and your compensation from your business. You should consult with a personal financial planner both before and after the sale of your business. You should also consider using a business financial planner to update and streamline your accounting operations.

The personal financial planner can provide valuable input in managing your personal assets before and after the exit. You need to have a financial plan in place for managing the lump sum payments you as the owner will receive at closing and over time as earn-out. That is, think through what you plan to do with the proceeds from the sale of your business. Your personal financial plan could impact how and when you will exit the business before and after the acquisition. Your personal financial planner can assist with the deal structure financial aspects and pay outs specifics, including the earn-out.

Business Broker

You should consider hiring an experienced broker to plan for the sale of your business. The business broker's job is to assist in identifying potential buyers and to be the liaison between the buyer and seller. The broker most often operates as would a stockbroker on Wall Street. Sometimes the broker and the exit plan advisor can be the same person, though that's not recommended. The broker might have knowledge of other similar deals, which will assist with valuing your business.

When we sold our first business, our business broker also played a key role in appeasing the principals—keeping them motivated and interested. He worked hard to keep the venture from imploding. He managed to present a unified venture management to the buyer and make the deal happen. The broker's compensation included an hourly consulting fee and the business sale's price commission. For example, the commission could be 10% of the first $1 million, 4% of the 2nd, and so on. We also covered all his travel expenses.

Accountant (Business Financial Advisor)

Choose an accounting firm that has small business mergers and acquisitions experience. Your accountant will be instrumental in helping you to decide what the intrinsic value of your business is, in collaboration with your business broker. The accountant will also support your exit plan by sorting out your business finances. He/she should be able to assist you with sorting out the fixed costs vs variable costs in your business and streamlining them. The goal is to have a lean operation with well-defined finances in preparation to sell your business.

Use your contacts and referrals to find your startup an experienced small business accounting firm. They can add value from early on. Often, the initial start-up accounting support comes from one accountant or a small firm.

In our first business, my father-in-law, who was an accountant, managed our books for a few years. When business picked up and revenue grew, we engaged the services of a large, local accounting firm. They both served us well.

Look for accounting firms that also have small business as well as large client accounts. They can assist you in setting up accounting systems online to make tracking and reporting your expenses, filing your taxes, etc. much easier.

In one case, our accounting firm saved me from personally paying significant ordinary income tax rather than capital gains tax.

Your accountant will likely recommend using accounting software. You need to adopt and use this option to save time and money in accounting data management.

Your accountant might also have valuable business contacts to connect you with.

Note: None of the examples and opinions provided in this book constitute tax advice. By using and relying on this book, you assume all risk and liability that may result.

Attorney

We often need the support of lawyers sooner rather than later. When you need a lawyer is *not* the time to go hunting around for a good one. You want to be sure your business is set up and run correctly—rather than discovering problems and snags when you are preparing to sell it.

Use your contacts to find and hire the best legal team, making sure they have small business startup service and mergers and acquisitions experience.

Your attorneys can act as both your internal and external regulator and support the entity to ensure compliance with regulations and terms and conditions of various agreements. This includes patent attorneys who are familiar with your area of expertise. Law firms also have many contacts that can come in handy.

I believe the primary use of attorneys should be to make sure your contracts are legal, binding, and with recourse in case of violations. However, *you* need to work out the actual terms and conditions of all deals. Negotiate the key points in the deals to your satisfaction, and then have the attorneys review for compliance.

In particular, always get legal assistance when preparing legal documents from a law firm experienced in contracts, including licensing and mergers and acquisitions.

You should seek advice from a licensed attorney before using or relying on this book.

Investment Banker (Broker)

You should consider hiring an investment banker (broker), depending on the business revenue and expected purchase price. We typically see deals over $50 million justify hiring an investment banker. They operate as a business broker finding buyers. They also have the financial expertise to assist with streamlining the business's finances for the acquisition process. Their fees tend to be much higher than a broker. Investment banker baseline fees, for example, could be 3 to 5% of the purchase price for $50 million deals. If the acquisition includes complicated financial structures, including stock swap and other financial arrangements, I think hiring an investment banker would be justified. Here again you would need to find an investment banking firm familiar with your industry.

Chapter 4
Using Your Business Plan

Usually, potential business buyers are provided with a business prospectus, followed by a detailed business plan. An important section within your business plan is the exit plan. (See Appendix F)

Most successful business owners have some form of an organic, living business plan. The business plan is used to raise funds and to provide a roadmap and focus for the management team. Business plans are continuously modified, based upon feedback from customers and lessons learned in the marketplace. The business plan helps to provide a clear unified vision, and it can be used to attract talent, make investments, and team up with other third-party entities. Your business plan should be easily understood by nontechnical people, including investors, customers, and ultimately the buyer of your company.

Key aspects of a business plan are the management team and extensive knowledge of the growth niche market you have focused on. The exit mindset should prioritize your efforts in various aspects of the business.

For example, initially, our first company had a 100-page business plan. We were offering multiple products and services for various applications in different industries. Eventually, we edited our business plan down to 20 pages for penetrating the growing fragmented semiconductor fabrication chemical market niche. We focused on one application in one market segment of the semiconductor fabrication industry. We cut out the extensive description of our various products and their advantages. We even dropped our profitable consulting service.

It took us five long years of meandering and pivoting to get there. After all, we had two brilliant scientist cofounders and me with many product/business ideas in three different, unrelated markets. But we had little understanding of any of these markets, so we dropped all but one product for one niche market.

In our first business, we pivoted a number of times. In the end, we focused our effort on the lowest hanging fruit, the new, fast-growing semiconductor fabrication industry niche: the wafer surface preparation process called contamination removal. We did that based on marketing information we gathered and acknowledging the limited in-house resources and marketing expertise we had. This change was afforded to us by support from a few venture capital firms and the Ben Franklin Technology Partners (BFTP-NEP) of Northeastern Pennsylvania, which was established in 1982 in Pennsylvania. The BFTP requires a short simple executive summary of the business plan to engage with a startup applicant, which is a good place to start. Their brief plan, referred to as the Venture Profile, covers all the key business plan segments. Each section has the same amount of space to write about.

This summary is on their website: https://www.nep. benfranklin.org. In Appendix A, you'll find their Venture Profile topics. You will note that they request to know your exit strategy. This writeup could be your executive business summary. Most of the information can be also included in your prospectus provided to potential buyers.

Chapter 5
Letting an Exit Mindset Drive Your Finances

When you have investors, throughout the life of your business, an exit mindset must drive your finances. The business financial matters need to be optimized. Quarterly, or bi-annually, you should work with your accountant on your financial statements, such as your profit and loss statements. Keep an eye on the profit margins. Make sure the overhead does not creep up.

Before you start thinking about selling your business, you must make sure you have a healthy net operating profit. To do that, you need to reevaluate your fixed and variable costs of doing business.

Minimize fixed costs that have a significant impact on your profit margin. Before selling your business, any fixed cost that has a return on investment (ROI) longer than 3 years needs to be avoided. You need to avoid large, fixed costs altogether, such as buying a building. If you need essential equipment, purchase used equipment or lease, rather than buying it. Only make purchases that are necessary to sustain and improve the business growth potential for the next 3 to 5 years.

For example, in my business, we reduced our fixed costs where possible by using services offered by other companies by outsourcing our operational and R&D needs. This helped to improve our financial position to optimize our exit value.

Let me give an example of a poor investment decision. In our second successful venture, I authorized the purchase of a $250,000 piece of lab equipment that my R&D team told me was essential. A few months after the purchase, when I visited the lab I noticed the piece of equipment was in the corner of the lab, covered up, and unused. When I questioned the lab team, they responded that the project they needed the equipment for was over, and they had no further use for the equipment! To me, that was a poor decision because I had not questioned the necessity of the purchase well enough. Instead of spending $250,000, we could have outsourced, rented, or leased that piece of equipment for a fraction of the cost to buy it. I call that a sunk cost.

On the other hand, variable costs include things like the building lease, staff salary, and your compensation before and after the acquisition. Once profitable, we tend to pay ourselves well, lease company cars, and award ourselves other perks. However, it is wiser to pay ourselves the going industry rates. As the business grows, pay bonuses rather than increasing salaries. Salaries should be in line with industry standards. Salaries must be competitive and are to be adjusted for inflation and promotions. Another perk to attract talent is to give stock options.

Then consider the cash reserve and other monies in company bank accounts. When we sold our second company, before the final terms and conditions of the acquisition were settled, we had significant cash reserves in the company's bank account. We therefore gave ourselves bonuses, arranged for social trips for the staff, and awarded other perks. Going into the negotiations, we still had approximately $2 million in our business account, which meant we were financing a portion of the buyer's purchase price of our business!

Chapter 6
Valuing Your Business and Technology

Before you begin thinking about selling your business, you need to have a good idea of its value. Ideally, you should always know the worth of your company. Your accountant can help with this.

At the end of the day, though, it does not matter what *you* think your company is worth. Ultimately, the value of your business is decided by the *buyer*, and you will then agree or not, depending upon how eager you are to sell.

Here we will focus on three of the many options to value a business selling price.

A: Present Worth Valuations

This method uses the potential growth in net sales revenue or Earnings Before Interest, Taxes, Depreciation, and Amortization (EBITDA) over the next few years using an interest rate to decide what the value of the business is at present. The net sales revenue is the method I used to decide what our businesses were worth, and in both cases the buyers paid more than the Present Value (PV) for our businesses. If they had offered less, I would have objected.

$PV=FV/(1+i)n$

Where:

PV = present value

FV = future value, (typically sales revenue in a certain year in the future)

i = interest rate per period in decimal form

n = number of periods (number of years)

Also this may be referred to in a different format as Discounted Cash Flow (DCF) valuation or analysis.

The buyer will resort to industry information on what is referred to as multiples as discussed below to compare PV compared to multiples on annual sales, etc. (See "Multiples on Annual Sales Revenue" below.)

You could use the EBITDA approach with your DCF method to estimate the worth of your business. But be cognizant of certain fixed and variable overhead expenses that can be reduced or eliminated. This action would improve the margins and add to your business value. I think its worth the time and effort to go down this path over time as you get your business ready for sale.

The acquiring company looks at your financial information differently than you do.

There are also opportunities for a larger firm to consolidate certain parts of your operations. For example, the buyer might have ample capacity to produce your product in-house, which will provide the buyer with significant additional savings. Another example is high salaries and bonuses paid to founders and key employees can be changed to fall in line with industry standards after the acquisition. You need to look for and be able to capture some of that as additional value in your negotiations.

B: Multiples on Annual Sales Revenue Valuations

Typically, the multiple is based on the industry segment your technology is sold to. But be aware, the multiple can be anywhere from 1 to 100. This is quite popular and utilized by buyers to justify the low price they are willing to pay. Simply, the buyer might use a multiple on your annual net sales or EBITDA to determine the purchase price. You must negotiate for a higher multiplier than what they propose by having done your homework. Push for a higher multiple based on future growth of the business and profitability.

Often, the venture's sales revenue has not reached a steady level. The sales growth is more in step fashion rather than a smooth curve. Have you considered and accounted for other applications your technology may be applicable for? Investigate the other divisions of the buyer for synergy and crossover of your technology.

In one case, a large multi-division firm bought a tech startup not because of the niche the startup was in—but rather for a much larger market niche that the founders were not aware of. The deal was structured such that the purchase price was based only on their small business niche. The founders left a ton of money on the table. This happens often because the buyer organization is typically a much larger multi-division operation. They have a much broader perspective of your technology application's crossover to their other niche applications.

C: What the Market Can Bear Valuations

This is the most important type of valuation!

Be aware, various methods and calculations can be used to justify a price on your business by the buyer, including those listed previously. However, when the deal is a strategic acquisition for the buyer, you can negotiate a much higher price. Strategic deals—such as buying your business because you have identified a hot growing niche, secured certain key accounts, and penetrated certain territories—make all the difference. These strategic acquirers are the buyers you should identify and invite to bid. Often, we underestimate the synergy that may exist with the other divisions of the buyer's organization.

When you are doing your exit plan valuation, shop for the best deal. Have at least two potential buyers come to the table and bid if possible. Let them know confidentially that they appear to be the lowest bidder.

My advice is to shop the sale and do your homework on

options A and B. Determine why the buyer is interested in acquiring your venture and how they see your company fitting in with their organization. What you learn might surprise you. Visit the buyer's company operations. Interview the buyer's staff and learn as much as you can about the buyer's organization, business, sales, and market presence in various accounts and territories.

Note, it's important to find out what motivates the buyer of your business. The buyer might be doing a strategic purchase, which has much higher value than a financial purchase. The lesson here is for you to attend the negotiations well prepared. Find out what your company is worth to them, not what *you* think is a fair price. Would you be satisfied with $10 million if the buyer could be willing to pay $50 million or more? Granted for most of us with humble beginnings $10 million is a fortune. But do not underestimate your business's worth. It's all about the impact your business will have on the buyer's company. You owe it to yourself and other shareholders to maximize out on the value of your business. Why should we let the buyer take advantage of our naivety?

Your exit plan adviser and business broker will be invaluable here. The broker will shop for buyers and identify the buyer with the highest level of interest. This arrangement can be very useful and cost effective. Most brokers have a list of contacts and depth of experience that will enhance your negotiation position.

Chapter 7
Negotiating and Closing the Deal

There can be several meetings in house and at other locations to sort out the sale of any business. Here are some simple tips for negotiating.

Do not do it alone. At a minimum, use an exit plan advisor, who can assist with much of the initial prep work and negotiations. Your exit plan advisor can manage the initial discussions with the potential buyers—so that you can stay focused on running and growing your business. (I wish we had an exit plan advisor. Fortunately, our business broker handled most of this work. We were quite naive selling our first business. We also were too engaged with our own internal conflicts among the owners.)

In absence of exit plan advisors, many business owners let their lawyers and business brokers take on all the negotiations. Some lawyers and brokers are qualified to do so. But I recommend you set boundaries. Limit the terms and conditions you are willing to allow the lawyers and brokers to work on and negotiate on your behalf.

Your attorney and accountants will be busy preparing the documents needed to make the sale.

Let these experts do their jobs. This is a time-consuming, intense, emotional, and frustrating period in your life. You need to balance the needs and wants of your co-owners as well as the buyer.

Require the potential buyers to submit their bids for your business within a fixed time frame. Require that the bids include the purchase price with terms and conditions, including earn-out and your role after the acquisition. **Never suggest what you will be satisfied with in money and terms**. Let them make the offers.

Be prepared: This might be a long, slow process. The exit process negotiations and closing of the deal could take 6 to 12 months—or even longer. The time it will take to make the deal will depend on the following.

- How well you have prepared and executed on your exit plan

- How well the co-owners are cooperating with the decision to exit and the process to exit

- How badly the buyer wants the deal done

- How much due diligence the buyer does. Part of the negotiation phase is due diligence, and the due diligence conducted by the buyer will take a while. They will want to see for themselves what your key accounts think of your business and the products they use. They will be looking for exposure, liabilities, and ways to minimize their risk. They want to ensure they can realize the goals they have set for your business after the acquisition.

Do not make a decision on a buyer until you have reviewed a few other bids, too, if possible. (We did not have any other bids even though we had a few other potential buyers.)

Let the potential buyers know there are other bidders.

Take lots of notes during the negotiations. Get to know the buyer's team members involved in the acquisition.

Be prepared to walk away from the first offer. That is, consider turning down the initial offer. I know, it's not easy to do when you see the money being offered.

When you receive the purchase agreement, read it and understand the terms and conditions well. Time invested at this stage—prior to signing—will save you much aggravation afterward.

Ask questions. Leave no room for misunderstandings.

Go over your notes and compare what was agreed to during the negotiation meetings with what is written in the agreement. Have your lawyer and accountant review the agreement and comment in writing with their thoughts and recommendations.

Include your exit plan advisor in the meetings and negotiations. Ask him/her to review and support your evaluations of the deal as presented in the purchase agreement.

Allow for and request adjustment clauses to resolve and handle performance issues and metrics established during the earn-out period.

Typically, the buyer will include clawback clauses to recover any costs due to incorrect information provided by the seller. The sellers need to include the same to ensure the buyer adheres to certain performance metrics. Also, clawback clauses are used to protect the seller from unforeseen events.

Look for clawback clauses by the buyer and minimize their financial impact on the deal. Include clawback clauses to protect your interests against events you have no control over.

Talk to other former owners of businesses the buyer has acquired.

Watch out for dishonest buyers (who are likely your competitors) backing out of the deal. (When selling our two businesses, we had the same competitor show interest but back out of bidding at the last minute. They took valuable, confidential data on our technology and business with them. This is a major reason why selling to your direct competitor should be your last resort.)

Once you are ready to sign, do not sign the final purchase agreement for at least 48 hours.

For more details on the purchase agreement see Appendices B and C for excerpts of actual agreements executed.

Chapter 8
Watching for Points of Contention

Common points of contention after the deal is consummated include the following.

Purchase Price

Multiple offers might assist you to learn and accept what the true worth of your business is.

In our case, we could have negotiated a higher price for our business. The multiplier used to determine our business's worth was too low. We did not insist on only 20% or less of the initial payment at closing to be withheld in an escrow account and not 30%.

Earn-Out Structure

Make sure you understand the terms for the earn-out. This includes the formula used and the years for which earn-out is paid based on sales revenue. Do the math. Negotiate the formula used and the percent allocated off the net sales to the earn-out.

In our first business sale, we had only 20% allocation.

Also, negotiate to extend the earn-out period. Typically, the earn-out period is 3 years. Why not 5 years? Why not for as long as your technology's sales are providing substantial revenue and profit for the buyer?

For example, you could negotiate a tapered earn-out structure after the first 3 years. In year 4, start at 10% of gross margin as earn-out. This payment would be tapered down each year, ending eventually at 1% of the gross margin.

In the fourth year after our second business was acquired,

our product's sales skyrocketed. Because our earn-out was limited to only 3 years, we did not see any earn-out for that significant spike in sales. A major client had qualified one of our products for their operation at R&D level at about the same time as closing of the deal. It took them a few years to build, equip, and operate their latest production line to full capacity. This client alone ended up purchasing $15 million per year of our product.

A Cap on Total Payment Including Earn-Out

Do not agree to a cap or at least raise the cap as much as you can on total purchase price, including the earn-out. I am not sure why there has to be a cap in the first place. It might be due to internal financing allocation at the buyer's organization.

After our first business acquisition, we reached the cap within the first 2 years. In the second deal, we did not reach the cap because the agreed to formula prevented us from reaching the cap.

Clawback Clauses

Clawback clauses can act as insurance policies in the event of fraud, misconduct, a drop in your business profits beyond your control, or poor performance by the parent company. You need to include the capability to review and confirm compliance by the buyer with the terms and conditions of the purchase agreement.

In one of our business sales, we had to fight hard to protect our product pricing. The buyer's organization at one of our key accounts was planning to use our product as a loss leader. They discounted our product pricing to generate more sales for their other divisions.

In another case, our technology application was denied promotion for another application—even though it had been verified. Another division within the buyer's organization refused to accept and promote our product within their division. We already had significant sales revenue from this other application for our products. We ran into internal Not Invented Here (NIH) syndrome at the buyer's other division.

Employment Agreements

Make sure you maintain as much control over your business after acquisition as possible. As a minimum, you need to be responsible for the Profit and Loss (P&L) of your business as a division of the buyer's company. Negotiate to operate your business as a separate division of the buyer's organization for as long as possible—at least as long as the earn-out period is set for.

Also, your pay and compensation, including benefits, must be at least in line with the division director level at the buyer's organization. If the buyer is an equity investment firm, you will need to negotiate based on your industry's salary and compensation surveys. However, you should always ask for more. It's all part of the negotiations.

Dispute Resolution

Even after all this negotiation and communication, disputes can arise. All disputes need to be settled though communication. Cool heads should prevail.

During my employment with the buyer company of the second business, there was a dispute among both parties' attorneys regarding the last earn-out payment to me. That dispute almost led to litigation. One evening, I was informed by our attorneys that they were heading to a federal court in Philadelphia the next day to litigate against the buyer of my business. I was surprised. I called my counterpart at the buyer's organization, and he was surprised, too. We settled the matter within five minutes and avoided a costly lawsuit.

If dispute cannot be settled in a friendly manner, the fall back should be arbitration—rather than litigation in a court of law. Arbitration takes less time and is much less costly than litigation.

Accounting Verifications for Future Payments

You must be able to independently verify the financial calculations made as to the accuracy of payments. The buyer might make it difficult and expensive for you to verify the numbers. If such disputes regarding the calculations arise, you must have reasonable recourse.

After my business was sold, we did not even consider challenging the earn-out payments over time. Here again, it was our mistake to trust the buyer's accounting.

Chapter 9
Licensing

Licensing is a business option that allows you to market your technology through a third party. Licensing is often unsuccessful. In fact, licensing is more of a challenge to the small business management than selling the business.

In some instances, an inventor/founder might prefer to license the invention because:

It is difficult to sell directly to the end user.

To reach certain market niches, such as the medical field, printed circuit board (PCB), and semiconductor fabrication industries, you might be requested to license your technology. The customer does not trust a small startup as a supply source. Licensing might take the form of territory exclusivity or application. In our case, two key potential customers requested we license our technology for them to use via a competitor who was their existing supplier.

Exporting and territorial coverage might require licensing. We did not have to license our technology to sell in Asia. We used manufacturer's representatives and distributors to reach customers in Taiwan, Japan, South Korea, and Singapore. The challenge here is the initial need for sales agents' training, joint sales, and technical sales calls on customers.

The invention is not a priority/focus to your organization since you have decided to pivot.

There are some upsides of licensing if managed well. Teaming up with another non-competing company in your niche by licensing your product/technology can be beneficial for the following reasons.

- They might have access, contacts, and knowledge of a market niche you are interested in.

- They might have more resources and knowhow to market to a specific niche.

- They are much better positioned to defend your technology against a competitor.

- Commercialization can be expedited.

- Licensing can provide much needed revenue early on based on the agreement terms and conditions as discussed above.

Prior to attempting to offer your technology/product for licensing, there is work to be done, including answering the following questions.

- Have you identified the application and in many cases also the other potential applications?

- Do you have proof of concept?

- How reliable is your data?

- Do you have endorsement based on third-party evaluations?

- Who are the potential licensees and why do they want to license?

- Do you have a patent or proprietary position on the technology? (Product with a patent is best.)

- How will you set the royalty payment rates? (Royalty could be anywhere from 5 to 25%. We had a 20% royalty payment arrangement.

- Negotiate to increase the royalty payment cap.

- What level of involvement will your team have in commercialization and scale up of the licensed technology? (You need to have plenty of involvement and oversight to ensure its success.)

- What if the licensee sits on the product and doesn't commercialize? (Have clawback or cancellation clauses to protect your business.)

When licensing your business or technology, there is disclosure of your valuable proprietary knowhow during the negotiations. The startup also loses control over the technology licensed and further development—without gaining full monetization. Prior to licensing, you need to make sure your product has a thought-out market plan and performance data needed to launch its successful commercialization. That way you can negotiate from a position of strength. Your licensing deal will be much more valuable when based on your tech's proven performance and market traction.

Licensing agreements must be thought through carefully—much like an agreement to sell your business would be. Licensing takes time, and it can be taxing on your time and focus. Make sure you understand why the licensee is interested and what application they are going to use it for. Be aware of what other applications potentially could make use of the technology. Here are some questions to consider.

Who should you license your product/technology to? For starters, not to the 800-pound gorilla competitor that dominates your market niche. In our fifth venture, we had this problem dropped in our laps, thanks to two of our potential clients wanting to have our competitor handle our product. Well, that did not work because the division head of our competitor said he was not willing to commit career suicide by promoting a competitor's product. However, they wanted to have their R&D team evaluate our product?!

Will the licensing be exclusive or non-exclusive? Limit by territory and application. Avoid exclusive licensing. If the licensee insists, negotiate based on the licensee's strengths in certain markets and territories. Have the licensee convince you they can and will commit the necessary resources to make it successful. Our first venture was saved by a non-exclusive license deal.

Generate some sales and land a few accounts before licensing. This market position greatly improves your negotiation position.

Licensing terms and conditions must be negotiated to include a significant lump sum upfront payment, when possible. This upfront payment is essential and intended to ensure the following.

- That the licensee is serious about the deal, has the resources to commit, and will work hard to generate sales to recover the upfront payment. Typically a six-figure upfront payment ensures the licensing agreement has been approved by the licensee upper management levels. A seven-figures upfront payment is even better.

- The licensor will then also have funds to ensure effective enforcement of the terms and conditions.

- The licensor gets value for disclosure of the technology and knowhow.

The technology information and your knowhow disclosed upfront are of great benefit to the licensee organization. This information will save them lots of time and money—millions of dollars or more. But more critical are the time savings and market timing. Businesses only thrive and experience rapid growth on discovering and capturing those windows of opportunity that pop up from time to time.

The licensee must pay for all those years of R&D efforts and product innovation you have invested in. Your market niche, proof of concept and how to sell to customers in this niche are also very valuable information. As the saying goes: Once the puzzle is solved, it's easy.

Should the licensee refuse to put up significant upfront funding, negotiate a partial repayment of the upfront fees against future royalties. In one licensing deal, I managed to secure substantial upfront and quarterly payments.

Lower upfront licensing fees might be agreed upon if and when you have confidence in your product prospects, having done your prospecting, and are assured of the licensee resources, commitment, and market position.

Insist on a minimum royalty payment guarantee, on a periodic basis, to ensure the licensee remains committed to invest in and promote your product/technology.

Insist on a performance/activity milestone structure by licensee. If the licensee does not perform, you must have the option to back out of the deal. Make sure you can get your technology back and the licensee has no further rights to the technology.

Secure ownership of any future development of the product or technology based on commercialization by the licensee or at least joint ownership. This item must be covered in the agreement upfront. Fight to keep ownership.

Make sure the termination clause and non-compete aspects of the licensing deal can be enforced by you at a reasonable cost.

The licensing deal must include a clause to allow you to verify the royalties owed at a minimum cost to you. You must have the ability to audit and verify your licensee's activities and payments. Most licensors neither insist nor exercise such options.

In Appendix D, see redacted portions of a Licensing and Technology Development Agreement we executed previously. At first glance, the deal appears to be an exciting, reasonable win-win deal. This was a unique agreement because it involved both licensing and joint development of products for a niche application that both our companies were active in. The agreement reflects some of the suggestions and advice in this book.

I was quite optimistic for the outcome of the agreement. The other company had previously bought a competing firm at a high price, and that deal had not generated the kind of return they had expected. So, they were eager to do business with us. We had been successful previously in our second venture to start, grow, and sell the business for the same market niche.

Unfortunately, the deal lasted only about two years before it was terminated by the licensee. They stayed true to the termination clause in the agreement. But they did not provide any reasons for terminating the agreement.

So, even with a good agreement, other elements can affect the outcome of any deal. The licensee could not break into the niche for which we had licensed our products. The agreement allowed them an expedited low-cost option to enter into a synergistic complementary market segment to their existing business for the same customers. They did commit resources, and they paid the minimum royalties due on time. However, the licensee was unable to dislodge the existing competitor's products.

Looking back, I believe the licensee got a better deal, considering the product information and knowhow they obtained in return for the licensing fee we received.

We did a poor job following up with the terms and

conditions of the agreement following the termination of the agreement. Because we were busy with other projects, we did not enforce our rights. I lost track of what we were supposed to follow up on to ensure full compliance of the licensee with the agreement post termination. There were requirements and obligations on both sides that lasted 10 years beyond the termination date of the agreement. They filed and obtained a patent on a new product. We should have been listed as co-inventor and co-owner of the patented product.

For further general details on licensing, I recommend *One Simple Idea* by Stephen Key.

Chapter 10
Management Team

The buyer of your business expects you and the other owners to leave soon after the acquisition—typically, within the first 2 years or even at closing. How will you prepare for that?

Consequently, the buyer is looking for depth of talent in the management of the business, who can keep things running after you leave. The buyer needs to see the business can operate well and grow without the founders and owners around anymore. How will you ensure that?

The answers to both of those questions need to be spelled out in your exit plan.

Often management is made up of the visionary/inventor—the person who had the initial a-ha moment and made the initial discovery of innovation or did the market gap analysis—and also cofounders, co-owners, talented managers, and board of directors. These are the people who will most likely be exiting the company after the sale.

Below that top leadership level, innovation can also be found in product/service development, market gap analysis, sales, manufacturing, and new applications for existing products. The buyer will look to retain many of your talented team members. After my departure from the second buyout, the buyer had my associates continue to manage the division.

Only few of the successful businesses I know and have read about are led by technologists who also are good at sales and marketing. Some can readily express the benefits of their offering to customers. In the early stages, often the founder needs to be both the inventor *and* the salesperson. A successful founder or cofounder is passionate about the business and understands the niche market well. But few founders fit this description. Also, there is not enough time in a day to do it—all by yourself. Therefore, over time you have likely established a strong, talented management team. At the least, you need a talented person managing each of your departments. This prevents you from having to micromanage your business.

In my second business, I had talented R&D scientists taking care of product development, while I handled the business marketing needs and other aspects of the business. The team included a former partner from my first business. However, I was still in charge of and very involved in our R&D efforts, making sure we stayed focused on immediate customer needs.

Exit Plan Buy-in

Hopefully, you know and trust your co-owners, management, and staff. And hopefully, your co-owners and management team are on board and agree with your goals—including the exit plan.

However, you should share your exit plan only with a few colleagues, and only on a need-to-know basis. This can be a tricky balance to find because you'll develop the exit plan over time through multiple meetings. And for a smooth successful exit, you need to develop the exit mindset. This is not easy to accomplish—nor easy to hide from other people in your company.

You need to plan for and spend the time to develop the exit mindset in your team. This is when your exit plan advisor can be very effective. You might wish to camouflage the process from most employees to prevent disgruntled employees from disrupting the deal. Using consultants can also prevent exit plan information leaking to employees.

Finding Management Team Members

The entity that buys your business needs to see that you have structured your business for continued growth and profitability—without you involved in day-to-day operations. This objective requires hiring and training talented staff who are passionate about the business.

As you might imagine, the time to find, hire, and train management team members is *not* when you are preparing to exit your business. You need to have your team in place, learning and growing, long before that.

You will find these future team members mostly through contacts and referrals. But by far the best sources to find talented team members are your competitor's top performing talents. This includes your previous employer's coworkers. Find experienced corporate staff who are willing to leave their dead-end jobs, have recently retired, been laid off, or have hit the glass ceilings in the corporate world. Also look for talent at technical conferences and trade shows and in trade publications. You will be surprised how many talented scientists, marketing, and sales staff of large corporations are willing to jump ship. Some want to take revenge on their boss and employer. They will be motivated to work hard and go the extra mile for your company.

You are looking for smart, motivated, committed, creative team members. How can you attract this top talent to your team—quickly? Offering them equity in a growing small business is very inviting. To attract and keep top talent, my businesses provided incentives and perks, including stock options for all employees. We gave bonuses, celebrated occasions, and recognized good performance.

The Challenge of Co-Owners

When organizing your business, avoid giving cofounders/co-owners equal equity shares and equal say in the management of the business. That is a recipe for conflict as the business grows and matures. If you already made the mistake of being equal co-owners, as you create your exit plan, try to work with your co-owners to modify the stakes in the company.

In our first venture, we agreed to equal shares of ¼ each among the four co-founders. That was a mistake—in my opinion. But I understand how co-founders think when they first get together and are excited about the startup. In my second venture, I kept the majority equity position and voting shares, which prevented any disruptions from disgruntled co-founders, investors, and key team members. I did have investors and employees as minority shareholders.

My favorite business analogy is the hunting Arrow (Bolt). Here's how the parts of the bolt symbolize the parts of a business:

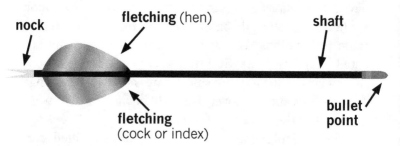

Nock: connections to finance

Shaft: the organization/staff

Arrowhead point: The product and/or service that can be changed based on target type, distance from the target, and other market conditions

Fletchings: The founder in charge (cock or index) and

management team (hen), including other cofounders who provide the guidance and focus.

One cofounder needs to be the arrow index. If the co-owners cannot agree on some key issues during regular office hours and not even at the board meeting, you have a serious problem. That is when the arrow index has to make the final decision. Articulate this in your exit plan.

Remember that a company officially (legally) has three officers: president, secretary, and treasurer.

All these other titles, including CEO, CFO, COO, vice president (VP), and many others, are additional titles given as the business grows. These are in my opinion not necessary.

Co-owners, mentors, and advisors (including consultants) must be a cohesive, well-rounded team with a single focus. Typically, at a minimum in a small business, you need the tech inventor as well as a marketing partner. If this is your first business, you also should add another cofounder or consultant who has entrepreneurship experience. Startup business experience is invaluable.

Before you plan to exit your business is the stop-and-regroup moment for the co-owners. Ask yourself: Is every co-owner on board with you on this decision? They need to be. It's common that when a new venture is struggling to get a footing and build a foundation, the cofounders usually pull together. However, trouble can surface once the business has gained traction and becomes successful and revenue, accolades, and awards become significant. This is when egos show up, and businesses face multiple points of contention.

As the business pivots, evolves, and grows, many co-owners disagree on focus, vision, and execution of action plans. Emotions can run high, and conflicts become disruptive to the business's future and survival. **Communication and compromise must see the team through these**

hiccups before they become fatal. As the business pivots and roles change, some co-owners might quit or need to be bought out. If your business is struggling with this type of issue, get help, including counseling and legal support.

For example, R&D cofounders might think their contributions are more critical to the success of the venture than sales and marketing—or vice versa. This is a fatal mistake. Many successful start-ups with initial market traction and a growing business succumb to internal disagreements. Co-owners become closer to each other than married couples. And we know the poor stats on marriages these days!

Our first business venture almost imploded because a cofounder fought for recognition of his perceived personal impact on the business and respective importance to the venture. The founders' egos and pride often get in the way of success.

To quote Benjamin Franklin from his book *The Way to Wealth* first published in 1758: "We are taxed twice as much by our idleness, three times as much by our pride, and four times as much by our folly."

I would modify the quote slightly differently as it applies to startup founder's behavior: "We are taxed twice as much by not delegating, three times as much by our pride, and four times as much by our ego."

Hopefully you have already decided each co-owner's role and assignments. That's easier said than done in the early days because founders wear many hats. As the venture grows, the founders will seek their comfort zones within the organization. However, they will fight to retain their decision-making powers. In the beginning, the inventor will promote his/her invention more passionately than anyone else. But the sales and marketing team must drive the business and manage the interactions of the R&D team with customers. Spell out each co-owner's role and assignments in the exit plan. For example, some team members might wish to part ways soon after the deal is done. But others might be required by the buyer to stay on.

Board of Directors

If your company has multiple owners and/or outside investors, you need to have a Board of Directors (BOD) that meets once a month—or more frequently as needed. Typically, your board should have an odd number of members, such as 5 or 7. An odd number ensures votes won't end in a tie. This info, too, should be detailed in your exit plan.

Hold board meetings regularly, especially after the business starts growing and becomes profitable. BOD meetings are essential to hash out issues that invariably come up. Keep a proper set of board minutes.

In our first business, we had 4 owners and also a 4-member BOD. Our board met monthly. The BOD saved my first business by managing cofounder disagreements. Prior to being bought out, we had our corporate legal counsel attend the last few board meetings to maintain order.

In my second business, I kept complete control of the business through stock ownership. I had learned my lesson. I did not need to hold BOD meetings. I only resorted to advisors and consultants as needed.

As you develop and implement your exit plan, rather than adding to your team, hire consultants to fill the gaps in your team. As mentioned previously, these include a personal finance advisor, business broker, accountant, and attorney. (See "Assembling Your Team" on page 22.)

Owner Buyout Agreements

No one is indispensable. Well, that is unless you own 100% of your own business. In our first venture, one of our co-owners quit and walked out. He returned a few days later when we did not agree to his outlandish requests.

Unfortunately, we did not have a buyout agreement for our first venture. That was clearly a mistake.

Similar to the need for prenuptial agreements before marriages, there needs to be an owner buyout agreement. Prenups require full disclosure of shared assets and articulate who gets what if the marriage ends in divorce. Owner buyout agreements do the same. This is a crucial part of your exit plan.

This code goes to a very informative Founder's Agreement Overview provided by University of Pennsylvania.

In my second business, I kept all the voting common shares and was the majority non-voting common shareholder. I therefore had full control of the second company and the rest of my businesses.

I cannot overemphasize the impact of adversarial relations that often develop among founders and co-owners. If these conflicts are not managed well, they can be fatal. They will have serious, negative impact upon the success of your business—especially the exit.

Buyout Agreements should prevent disruption to the business. (See Appendix E for information provided on this topic.) Cofounders' needs and founders' interests change over time. As you face pivoting moments, you will find some founders resist change and can become disruptive. There will be only the following two options.

- They fall inline.

- They leave using the buyout agreement.

The board of directors must decide.

For my first business, we did not have a buyout agreement, but fortunately we did have a board of directors.

We suffered, and we were very lucky to get bought out just in time.

It's important to note that the co-owners you start the business with might not be the same co-owners you exit the business with. As you grow the business, you will find some founders are not happy with changes made and their changing roles in the business. In some cases, you just cannot appease a cofounder. That is when buyout contracts can smooth the way through transitions and save the business.

Chapter 11
Understanding Your Market

Identifying an unmet niche market need as well as developing the solution to meet the need, are both extremely valuable to large companies—and to potential buyers of your company. Typically, large companies are not market pioneers. At best, they are fast followers.

Gather market info from various sources, such as the following.

- Your potential customers (Ask about their usage rate of the existing competitor's products.)
- Publicly traded competitor's published data, such as 10K and the annual reports.
- Industry journals and magazines
- Research papers
- Patent applications and issued patents
- News media
- Internet
- Other suppliers of complementary products to the same potential customers
- Suppliers (Often you and your competitors purchase from the same suppliers.)
- Friends and contacts directly or indirectly working at your competitors
- As a last resort: Hire a consulting firm or buy their reports on the market.

This is the time to tap into services offered by various federal, state, and local entities that are set up to assist small businesses. However, in many high tech niches, there is limited public information available. That was the case with our ventures. In the 1980s, the Small Business Administration (SBA) office we contacted had very limited market information on the new semiconductor fabrication industry.

How well do you know the niche market for your product/service? The buyer of your business is most interested in this knowledge. **Ideally, you need to operate in a niche, growing, fragmented market,** which is defined as a market that no single supplier/competitor dominates (having greater than 60%).

Your exit plan must demonstrate your knowledge and command of your market. This is the surest way to attract multiple potential buyers and maximize your payout.

Market intel must drive the business based on customer feedback and full knowledge of your competition's strengths and weaknesses. The growth and profitability of the business rides on this assessment.

Is your focus a niche market? Often a niche market is a small portion of a large growing market with room for new, small players with novel products. We were fortunate to have finally found and focused on such a niche market. In our first two businesses, after pivoting a few times, we focused on the fast-growing semiconductor fabrication industry market in the late 1990s/early 2000s. For our third venture, the growing solar cell industry was the initial focus. The focus of our fourth and fifth businesses was the shrinking, mature Printed Circuit Board (PCB) fabrication industry market, which forced us to pivot. You need to focus on growing markets—or at least stable ones.

Investors will become most interested in buying your business when you can prove you are in a niche, fragmented, growing market. The business value potential should be based on a growing profitable niche. That is how the recent startup unicorns managed to convince investors to invest at pre-revenue stage and value their startups in the billions of dollars!

It is not always easy to predict and time your entrance into a growing market. Some lucky entrepreneurs stumble onto a niche growing market. Others discover—or should I say uncover—such a market by accident. However, a niche new growing market typically has limited public information available. These markets could be in the United States, but more frequently they are in Asia. There are opportunities to grow businesses in a mature stable market by offering novel products to meet certain needs.

Let Market Intel Drive the Business

Our lesson learned was that finding your market is more important than the novel product/service you have invented. It does not matter what you have invented, if there is no market for your product.

There has to be a rapidly growing market in a growth niche for your product with barriers to entry. Or as in our fifth venture, your offering could be considered a "bleeding edge technology" in a declining mature industry. When we entered the printed circuit board fabrication industry, we had limited market knowledge. We ended up finding out too late that we were also competing against dominant competitors. The industry is slow in adopting new technology. We should have pivoted sooner.

In our first business, for a few years we meandered among different industries and market segments. As we gained more market feedback, we pivoted. In our second venture, we had focus from day one. We knew the niche semiconductor market well. We had customer contacts, and we were fortunate to have good timing with our customer's adoption of an upcoming new technology. They had to make changes to their existing process steps, adopting a new process in their semiconductor fabrication operations. They switched from aluminum to copper substrate as the current conductor in the electronics device called the chip. We were aware of this up-and-coming change, and we timed our entry well. It took us only three years to become very profitable and grow rapidly.

If you do not know your customer (the end user), get help early on. Attend conferences and meet and hire sales and marketing staff who do. In our first business, we eventually hired a marketing consultant. We mostly learned about the industry from our licensee. In the early 1980s, there was little public market information on the semiconductor fabrication industry.

It's important to ask yourself: Is your business market-driven or technology-driven? The entity considering buying your business wants to see a market-driven business that's supported by novel, cost-effective technology. Does the market drive your business development and focus? Does your organization demonstrate agility to take advantage of the windows of opportunity in a timely fashion? The key advantage that small businesses have over large established firms is agility. You must be able to commercialize a product when customers are looking for and need to use a new product. Do not wait for your R&D team to decide when the product development is complete to their satisfaction. Let the customer decide and use your product!

Obviously, your growing business is successful because you have already effectively met these very needs. Therefore, you are able to persuade your customers to pay top dollar for your product/service. Hence, you expect the buyer of your business to pay top dollar for the business and to allow your business to operate independently after the merger.

Identify Your Customers

The entity that wants to buy your business wants to know the answers to the following questions, so these should be spelled out in your exit plan.

- Do you have access to multiple customers for your product/technology?

- Does your offering save your customers time and money?

- Does your product solve a performance issue that existing competitors' products do not?

- What is their purchasing process cycle? (Some sales involved multiple customer departments and take up to a year or more to close.)

- What percentage of your customers are repeat customers?

- Do you have long-term contracts with customers?

Adding Value with More Than One Market for Your Products

Having more than one market for your products can add value to your business in the exit deal negotiations. However, that's only as long as it's properly detailed in your exit plan.

More often than not, there is more than one potential application or market niche for your products/technology. But how do you qualify and choose the low hanging fruit? Marketing efforts must determine how to choose the niche you will focus on initially—based on resources needed, access to customers, profitability, growth potential, timing, and barriers to entry. **Let the market decide.**

In one business consulting assignment, I came across a specialty chemical business that was up for sale. The business had market share in three different markets. At first, it might seem appealing that they had three markets for their products. But then we discovered they did not have a *significant* market share in *any* of the three markets they were selling to. The markets also did not overlap in technology utilized. The buyers walked, and the business was finally sold for its assets—rather than a stock purchase.

However, having other potential synergistic market niches for your core competency and potential technology crossover can greatly increase your business's value to a potential buyer. You need to investigate these potential overlaps as part of the exit plan. Sometimes a buyer is more interested in *other* markets your technology can be applied to—rather than or in addition to the markets you are currently operating in.

Capitalize on Multiple Potential Novel Products

What if you have a few novel products in your R&D pipeline for the same niche? Your exit plan needs to address this opportunity for future growth potential for the business. The exit plan can claim multiple applications in the same niche that add value to your business. You should consider providing proof of concept demonstrations for these other products in different market niches. Make sure you negotiate these into asking for a higher valuation of your business. The potential buyers might be well aware of these other crossovers of technology potential. They might not disclose these opportunities, which could multiply the value of your business!

This scenario can lead to licensing—rather than selling the business. Licensing is an alternative to selling a business. Licensing can allow another company to market your products. These other entities could be better positioned to promote your products by territory or applications. (More on licensing in Chapter 20.)

Understand Your Competition

The buyer of your business will certainly want to know how well you know your competitors and how you out flank them. You'll want to provide as much information about your competitors in your exit plan as you can. You need to list their strengths and weaknesses.

Have the utmost respect and fear for your competitors. They are watching your every move. So, practice camouflage. Hide your business activities and find ways to keep your competitors in the dark.

- Use stealth: Delay the detection of your venture's presence and technology.

- Divert attention: Advertise a different technology for a different application.

- Keep quiet: Do not publicize your best product early on.

- Be agile: Your objective is to continue to outflank and outmaneuver your competitors.

- Offer discounts (only if absolutely necessary): Your competitors might offer discounts to keep you out of the market, and perhaps they can afford to do that. You should not—unless you play along to force your competitors to lower their prices and decrease their margins at their existing accounts.

- Be paranoid: Being paranoid about your competitors will save your business from competitor's efforts to sabotage your business and allow you to grow faster. Sabotage takes many forms. For example, we had a competitor pretending to want to buy our business. They managed to have us hand over to them, on a silver plate, all our technology, know-how, and business information—only for them to not bid. When that strategy did not work, they threatened us with patent infringement. They are a Fortune 500 company.

Let's not forget large corporations' profits depend on the following three things.

- Luck

- Efficiency

- Collusion: When fortune collides with crime.

As French writer Honore de Balzac wrote: Behind every great fortune there is a crime.

While luck and efficiency might help initiate wealth, the capital system tolerates connivance, making Balzac's statement more plausible than it ought to be. Consider checking out this link to chapter 10 in the book *Capitalism Beyond Mutuality*.

What does connivance mean? "The verbal act of agreeing. (law) tacit approval of someone's wrongdoing. synonyms: secret approval, tacit consent"—*Oxford Languages Dictionary*.

Here's an example of connivance. Tucker Corporation, a new automobile company, was pushed into bankruptcy by the Security Exchange Commission (SEC) and the three auto companies in 1950 on fraudulent charges. Tucker's cars had many new designs, including car seat belts, shatter-proof glass, and fuel injection. His novel designs and safety features made the cars very popular before even selling one car. There is a movie called *Tucker*, and books, including this one, claim collusion of the auto companies with the government officials to destroy their competition.

Let's review what great Chinese warrior and philosopher Sun Tzu wrote in *The Art of War*:

- Strike at the weak and not the strong enemy.

- Know your enemy (Strength and Weaknesses, back to SWOT).

- Know yourself and your enemy better.
- Outthink your enemy; use guerilla warfare.
- Use deception and disinformation to mislead your enemy.

A top priority in my business is to study our competitors and watch their every move in product and marketing development. We review their patents, published technology papers, conference presentations, and journal articles. We look for ways they market and pitch their products, and we learn how to outmaneuver them.

We learned a lot from our competitors in various aspects of our ventures, including R&D and marketing. We were always on the lookout for our competitors' patents, new products, and product development information. We learned to practice "Beg, Borrow, or Buy." As part of our R&D efforts, we always benchmarked our products against our competitors' products. We made every effort to get our hands on our competitors' product samples.

Your competitor is your best teacher. Swallow your pride and learn from others, including your competitors.

Who is your competitor? Competitors come in many forms and shapes. They could be offering a similar product to yours or a disruptive technology to solve the same problem. They can be a division of a large corporation and therefore hopefully lack agility. Typically, your potential customers are using a competitor's product that you attempt to replace.

Spend time early on identifying your main competitors—especially the 800-pound gorillas. If you can demonstrate how you outperform them, you will ensure the growth of your business for years to come.

Look for ways to avoid head-on competition early on against your competitors. You don't want to give them the opportunity to learn too much about your business and products.

Keep a low profile and work in stealth mode as long as you can. It's best to generate market share with second or third tier smaller customers before you call on the top tier clients. The larger first tier customers are typically well attended to by your direct competitors. Your potential customer's staff is well connected to your competitor's staff.

Be on the lookout for your competitors' attempts to sabotage your efforts at customer sites and steal your information, including getting their hands on your products. Whenever possible, early on, have your potential clients sign a Non-Disclosure Agreement (NDA) before sending them your product to evaluate. Your valid argument can be that your technology is patent pending, even if it's only a provisional patent. Some larger potential customers will also ask for NDAs to protect their information. This might be an opportunity to set up a mutual NDA and get more involved with a potential client. (See information on Patents in Chapter 16.)

Rest assured that your competitors will do what they can so that your startup with a novel competitive product does not get a chance to gain market share. If their attempt to prevent the introduction of a competitor's new product fails, they will resort to other means. The competitors do whatever it takes to make sure a new novel product does not penetrate their niche—at any cost. For example, they might sue your business on patent infringement or call OSHA and other federal and state organizations on you under false pretense.

Here is an example of how well connected your competitors might be with some of your future potential clients. We recently had our product tech demo in China at a large manufacturing operation. We heard the initial results from our competitor before we heard from our own sales and tech representatives! The feedback from the competitor was false! The demo was successful, and we went on to present the results at an industry conference.

Here's a final word about your competition. Be on the lookout to attract top talent from your competitors to join your team. Talent adds significant value to your business.

Adopt a Sales Strategy

In large potential client firms, the people who buy your product (purchasing) and the people who will use your product (the end users) are usually two different teams with different priorities. This is when understanding your market niche will make all the difference. Often winning an account requires meeting various customer department's requirements, including the actual end user within the customer organization. At some large accounts, the purchasing agent is the gate keeper. For example, you might have to go through the client's buyer to set up meetings with the process engineers who are the end users of your product.

If you are not sure who your end user is, team up with someone who knows. That person should then hold a key management position. If not, hire a consultant to start with until you hire a very experienced, well compensated, key sales and marketing team member. This person will be responsible for focusing the business product development. The co-owners and CEOs of some of the most successful start-ups are experienced sales and marketing people who are well connected in the niche markets upon which they are focused.

Reaching the Early Adaptors

The early adaptors drive the industry's evolution by being risk takers who are willing to test startup company products. They are typically young engineers and scientists out to make a name for themselves. Often, they are impatient with their more senior coworkers who are no longer risk takers.

In our first few ventures, thanks to our sales representatives, we knew our customers and their purchasing procedures well. Our sales reps had good connections, and they prequalified the accounts before we called on them.

In our fourth venture, which was a new market for our technology, we did not know our customers and their purchasing procedures. We paid the price for it.

To identify and nurture your customers, I recommend you use a sales funnel. Typically, businesses go through multiple steps to secure a new account. Even though there might be hundreds of potential accounts out there, you need to get them into the funnel. You do that by making contact and convincing them to evaluate your product/service.

Here are the steps that applied to our sales efforts once we had made the initial contact and the customer was engaged.

1. Customer sample received
2. Testing conducted in-house
3. Testing conducted at Original Equipment Manufacturer (OEM)
4. Testing conducted at customer site
5. Successful initial qualification
6. Pilot use
7. First customer production order
8. Third repeat order, considered to be a "house account" (It took until the third order for the customer to get the feedback on the impact of our product on their product efficiency.)

These steps were needed to secure a new account in industry niches we were active in for our various ventures.

You need to ensure each segment of the sales funnel has an equal number of customers involved. This is reassuring to the business buyer, who wants to see an organized sales strategy to ensure continued growth of the business.

In my businesses, whenever we succeeded in getting a potential client past step 2, it increased the potential to secure their account to 20%. That is, we landed one out of five accounts! By the time we got an account interaction past step 4, we had a 75% chance of closing the deal. This data is essential to include in your exit plan.

Remember: Only the repeat customer (the house accounts) revenue, feedback, and contacts ensure your long-term success. That is what the buyer of your business is looking for.

Do not celebrate a new account until multiple orders have been placed, fully qualified, and used repeatedly by the customer. **You want repeat business**.

In our first venture, we lost an account after the first production order was placed and our product was used. Subsequently, it took our new customer 3 months to close the loop on full evaluation result and impact of our product on their finished product. Apparently, the result was not satisfactory, and they stopped purchasing any further product from us.

While sales team members can collect data and negotiate prices, marketing management sets pricing boundaries. There needs to be a floor on pricing that the salespeople cannot lower the price below—without convincing the marketing department to lower the price. **You must maintain a healthy profit margin**. Investors and business buyers look for solid, sustainable profit margins.

Product Champions

Who are your product's champions in your customer's organization? They are members of a customer organization who are supportive of your company, and they often can influence the internal customer events in your favor. They can also provide you with intelligence.

In a few cases, our product champions moved on to other potential client companies, and then they enabled us to penetrate new accounts. You need to take care of these champions and make them look good at their jobs.

Sales Projections

You need to estimate the sales revenue of your offering for your business plan. Initially it's going to be just an estimate. Investors/buyers will ask for such data to decide on the venture's present worth. Project your sales revenue based on previous year's sales revenue and growth potential as well as competitor's information. So, the more marketplace data you have, the more reliable your projections will be. Info on existing competitors' pricing and product usage will also enable you to make a more reasonable estimate of future sales figures. In one case, this knowledge enabled us to raise our prices.

When making your sales projection, please DO NOT use the method of claiming to capture a percentage share of the total market. That is, do not estimate your sales based only on market size for your product. For example, you wouldn't want to claim to capture 5% of a billion-dollar market in the next 2 to 3 years. This approach shows a lack of business experience and should be avoided. It often disappoints, and it might even turn investors off.

Instead, you need to estimate your sales based upon one customer usage at a time and build up your estimated future sales from there. You should also use competitor's sales revenue data to estimate your future sales.

Use the 80/20 Rule

The 80/20 rule is a principle that states 80% of all outcomes are derived from 20% of causes. It's also known as the Pareto Principle.

It's amazing how often in most businesses 20% of the clients make up 80% of the revenue. Yet, having only a few customers makes the investors and the buyers of your business very nervous. Your job is to make sure no one customer makes up more than 20% of your business revenue. Initially, that will not be the case. In early days, one or two clients will inevitably make up more than 80% of your sales revenue. That's okay. But as soon as possible, expand your sales to other clients. In the meantime, provide your key accounts with superior customer service.

Given the choice, call on second and third tier customers before calling on your top tier potential customers. There are lots of optimizations in product development and marketing including pricing, which are best dealt with at smaller accounts. These smaller accounts are usually eager to adopt new technology to grow their businesses faster. You can reach decision makers more readily, and it typically costs less to convince them to evaluate your product.

Choose Your Initial Customer Contact Strategy

Decide upfront who should be promoting and selling your product or service. You might be fortunate if you already have a potential client engaged in supporting your efforts in developing a needed technology. But that does not happen often. On the flip side, you need more than one or two accounts to grow a business.

Based on our first-hand experience, there are at least two serious concerns to think through on who should sell for you, what technology information should be shared, and at what stage.

Do not give out too much info. Inventors and founders tend to give out too much information in early stages of sales calls on a new account. They are too excited about their invention, and it does not take much prodding for the inventor to divulge far too much proprietary information. Remember: There are two parts to each product offering. One is the product, and the other, more important part is the knowhow. How to use the product (processing conditions) can at times be more important than the product itself. Sometimes your potential client can learn how your product is used and make their process work better using your competitor's product. Initially, your potential client has no loyalty to your startup. Often to try something new, the potential customer's staff needs to be desperate and out of time. They might have given up on the existing supplier's support to overcome a process challenge. This information should be reported to marketing to rank the potential. This scenario is usually the case with a change in the customer's process. They might need to adopt a new process or tool to produce a new product, etc.

Do not trust the new potential client. A new customer's staff might request your technology info—only to pass it on to your competitor. How many times have you convinced an existing account staff to gather information from your competitor? How many times have you pretended to be a potential client? How many times have you contacted a competitor asking questions?

Initial sales calls are exploratory calls to judge how interested a potential client is in your technology. During the call, you have the opportunity to gauge how loyal the client is to your competitor, which is the client's current supplier of a competing product. It's best that you send experienced salespeople to that initial intro meeting to gauge potential client interest. Let the sales staff qualify the account first before getting too excited. There are many potential accounts your team could call on. Have your salespeople screen them as well as they can.

Remember: Be paranoid. Make sure that your sales staff does not pass too much valuable info onto your potential customer nor leave behind any proprietary data. In fact, you should *expect* the potential client to tip off your competitor about your company, technology, and any other info you unwittingly share. It happened to us during our fourth venture—twice.

Your sales staff must regulate the disclosure of information to potential clients at the early stages of qualifying an account. Their job is to evaluate the account for the marketing team. Then the marketing team decides if the account should be placed into your sales funnel. Once the marketing team has prequalified the account, bring out the big guns—the inventors and R&D folks on your team.

Prequalifying an account means determining they have the budget to purchase your technology or are willing to make the necessary modifications to their existing operating set up to use your product. Tech product sales take time and are expensive. Generating the data to win over a new account can cost millions of dollars. Sales staff calling on customers must use a checklist to submit to marketing to evaluate and list potential accounts to call on based on level of interest and trust. Such sales and marketing procedures will show the investors and the buyer of your venture a professional, well-managed organization that will continue to grow.

It's important to keep in mind that a major obstacle for a business to overcome when selling a new product is the reliability of the supply source. The recent experience with supply chain interruptions has made the situation worse. Customers prefer to purchase from large established suppliers.

Many times, I've heard the statement, "We like your product, but your firm is too small." It's worse still when a potential customer says, "License your product to our existing supplier or a big firm." But it pays to consider that advice because that's when licensing your technology might become a viable option.

In two cases early on in my businesses, our potential clients introduced us to our biggest competitors! We met and negotiated with our competitors. These discussions did not end well. So much for stealth mode of operation.

So, screen and prequalify the potential accounts you plan to call on.

Excel at Customer Service

Customer service generates invaluable loyalty and trust. Your business is built on repeat customers. And repeat customers is something a potential buyer for your company is really looking for.

Make customer service a high priority. Improve your business credibility with *superior* customer service.

It is much easier and much less expensive to grow your business with an existing client than by landing a new account. Offering superior customer service ensures repeat business and long-term relations. Customer service often opens more doors for your business.

In a few cases, our product was qualified and being used in one customer production line, and that was soon followed by adoption at their other operations around the world using our product. Our customer's staff began asking us to support their efforts as they introduced our product to their other operations. Those engineers are our product champions.

We also have had cases when the customer's staff asked us if we could supply other products as well. Those product champions provided us with invaluable information, feedback, and ideas.

If you are looking for examples of excellent customer service, visit Wegmans supermarkets and Home Depot stores and watch Amazon in action. Their service is unparalleled. Almost every time, I'm surprised by their staff's professionalism, training, and response. Customers keep coming back and buying from these companies, which explains their rapid growth. Therefore, they can charge a premium and enjoy very healthy margins. Wegmans is also repeatedly listed as one of the top five best places to work. The level of staff training at Wegmans is impressive. The quality of their products is also very high.

It is better to under-promise and over-deliver—in other words exceed your customer's expectation. That is how you win customer loyalty.

Many times, I have seen salespersons over-promise what they can offer but then under-deliver. They exaggerated what they can deliver and what their product can do for the client—only for the client later to find out that is not so. That's the surest way to lose credibility. The fastest way to lose future business is to offer things you cannot deliver.

We referred to one of our vice president's sales strategy as a "customer burn list." He was very good at getting the *first* order from a new customer—but no repeat orders. He oversold the product offering and quality, and then the product fell short of the customer's expectations. The customers would not call him back to buy more from him.

One of the worst experiences I had in business was sitting across the table from the president of a client in the conference room of a large semiconductor fabrication operation in Taiwan, facing his wrath. Our sales team had promised a certain date for the delivery of our products, which were months behind schedule. Our business had too many orders to fill, and we could not deliver on time.

Blending Disruptive and Sustaining Technology-Based Products/Services

Once your business is up and running profitably, you need a mix of both sustaining and disruptive products. What do these two terms mean?

Do you have a product looking for a market? That's disruptive.

Or do you have a market looking for a product? That's sustaining.

A disruptive product can also be called pioneering or even bleeding-edge technology. Does your offering require changes to the existing mode of operation? Does your product or service require significant customer resource investment and changes to the present mode of operation by the client?

Or is it a sustaining technology (improvement on existing technology in use), which would typically need minimum effort on behalf of the end user to adopt. Can your product replace the competitor's product in their existing process as a drop-in replacement by saving them time and money?

Start marketing first with a novel, sustaining product. That is responding in time to existing windows of opportunity.

A sustaining product/tech offering that solves your customer's immediate needs can open doors. Sustaining products can generate revenue faster, and they need fewer resources. Sustaining products provide you with a calling card to allow you to penetrate accounts early on and engage with your product's end users. Sustaining products also allow you to get to know your market upfront and get much needed feedback. You can then develop and introduce your disruptive technology.

Sustaining tech innovation usually requires much less time, resources, and effort to get traction in the marketplace. Look for windows of opportunity. They do not stay open for long.

In our first venture, we quickly learned to ride the coat-tail of our competitor's market positions. My cofounders had recently left this competitor's employment, right before we teamed up to start the business. We called on the competitor's accounts where the products we were attempting to replace were invented by one of our cofounders. We had patents to prove that. Therefore, we had instant credibility with those clients. Our product performed slightly better and had demonstrable benefits over the existing Process of Record (POR) competitor's products.

Sustaining products can also be crossover technology from one application to another within the same production line. We have been successful in crossover of our core technology from one application to another in the same industry and other similar processes in other industries. In our second venture, we knew there was a pending production process change by our clients. That is, there was a new market opportunity looking for a product. Because of our credibility due to our success with the first venture and contacts, we were able to engage with potential customers and their production equipment suppliers who were evaluating products for their new processes.

On the other hand, disruptive technology takes a long time to become a commercial success—sometimes years! Disruptive technology requires educating the end user, significant change in the customer's production process, and the logistics to support the technology. But the perceived value of the disruptive technology often allows you to secure significant higher prices for your products than sustaining technology.

SWOT Analysis

When identifying your market, the Strength, Weakness, Opportunity, and Threat (SWOT) analysis is a useful tool to learn and put into practice. It's also important to include this analysis in your exit plan. Large businesses, investors, and potential buyers are often interested in the seeing SWOT analysis of your company and using it to learn more about your business.

If you do not have the time for the full SWOT analysis, just conduct the O and T parts. They are the two most important steps, so I prefer to call it the OTSW analysis. The O and T sections of the SWOT tool might be useful in identifying the low-hanging fruit product/service for your business—where there is likely less competition.

In retrospect, I am not sure we knew how to formally practice this form of analysis. Where we constantly did practice the S and W part of the SWOT was on studying our competitors' strengths and weaknesses. In particular, we successfully went after our cofounder's previous employer's customers. In one case, we discovered that the customer was using one of our cofounder's inventions in their production line.

Let's talk about each letter of OTSW.

Opportunity: This is the a-ha moment, your vision! How can you describe your product/services and its benefits? (Remember not product features. Customers are looking for benefits to be spelled out to save time and avoid confusion.) How does your invention solve your potential customers' problems? What is your competitive advantage?

Threats: This includes your competition, regulations, timing, location, and logistics. Never underestimate your competition, both direct and indirect. Also, regulations can slow and or even kill your business. Timing is everything. Location of your customers is key.

Strengths: These might include your expertise and experience in R&D, marketing, and contacts.

Weaknesses: These could be lack of expertise and experience in marketing, R&D, negotiation skills, funding, or lack of contacts.

Set Your Pricing

This is another key aspect of your business marketing. Pricing is often initially calculated based upon multiples of total cost of product production. This is an easy approach, and it does not require conducting market studies. Founding technologists/scientists often are not skilled in marketing, negotiating, nor pricing. Often, the multiple of costs to set prices approach is too simplistic, and it could lead to lower profit margins.

Pricing must be based on what the market can bear. Set your prices based on the benefits your invention provides. In one case, our product performance improved the efficiency of the client's product by 1%, and it enabled our client to win over their coveted customer account.

To set a price, gather the following.

Feedback: Gather feedback from your customers. For example, the client engineers involved in qualifying our product gave us the confidence to negotiate pricing our product from a strong position with their buyer. We did not discount our price. We did not relent under the purchasing agent's repeated demands and threats. But we did appease him by proposing future discounts on higher volume purchases and performance data exchange.

Competitor product prices: Your competitor's prices can often set the price elasticity.

In our first venture, we initially agreed to low pricing of our products to our first large key account. We were desperate, and we lacked market information. We wanted to gain market share, and we needed to generate revenue—at any cost. (Fortunately, we survived this poor strategy.) Later, we discovered our competitor's pricing was much higher than ours—to the same customer.

Watch for large potential customer's purchasing office's negotiation games. Yes, negotiating price is a game you must learn to play. The secret to winning is to negotiate about more than price—have other gambits, such as purchase volume and inventory levels.

However, your product pricing should allow for some discounting to purchasing agents so they can justify their jobs and secure future promotions.

In one case, we had to provide 5% discounts to each of the customer's purchasing agent, his boss, and his boss's boss. But the next time we sold that customer our products, we increased our prices by 20% entering negotiations to reflect this discounting play by the customer's purchasing office.

Your sales agents can and must also provide competitor's information, including usage and pricing information to the marketing team. In one case, our sales agent convinced us to set a higher price for an Asian client.

Gross margin (GM): Gross margin % = (sales price - cost)/ sales price. With experience, we were able to raise the GM from 30% to 85% by setting higher prices for our products. We became very profitable. GM review is a useful tool to use to set prices and ensure you have good margins on a product-by-product basis.

Know When to Discount

Even after you've set your price, you're not finished. You have to consider: Is there room for discounting?

Negotiate on a dollar amount discounting—rather than percent discounting: Percent discounting has a much larger impact on your margins than discounting using $$. For example, if you agree to a 5% discount off a $100 price, that's a $5 discount, when the buyer might have been satisfied with a $1 discount.

Price is not the only way you can discount. Look for ways to lower your costs—not just your price and secure longer term purchasing contracts. For example, in one case we convinced a client to allow us to change our product packaging container's size and shape and to ship in larger containers and in larger volumes.

Investors and your company's potential buyer are very interested in your firm's sustainable profitability based on high gross margins. Also, you can recover from mistakes and crises only if you have healthy margins. If your prices are too low, any product rejection, recall, or unexpected costs can swallow up any profits.

Also, never negotiate only on price. There must be other parameters (gambits) included in the negotiations, such as quantity, packaging, and shipping costs. (See "Negotiations" on page 35 for lessons about this we learned on the job.)

Price high, knowing you are going to discount. It's much easier to discount prices from a high price position than asking to raise prices later.

Maximize your profits through effective pricing. You need to negotiate well and hold the line when dealing with customers and suppliers. Small businesses cannot afford the Loss Leader approach. This approach is used by large established firms attempting to gain market share and keep competitors out.

Marketing must set prices, but they must be based upon feedback from the sale steam. Your sales team must be given a price list based on unit/volume/frequency, etc. Any deviation from the price list must be approved by marketing.

Do not discount pricing of your product/service to gain market share. If you have to compete on price, you will give up your precious profit margin. That is not how to grow a successful, profitable venture. Low profit margins will reduce any interest from third-party mergers and acquisition potential partners. A potential buyer will investigate both the net sales revenue and profits.

In another business consulting project, I noticed the

profit margins were minimal. They were in the waste recycling business—a mature market. The technology implementation, recycling spent acids, was difficult and hazardous. The recycling business is a low-margin business, subject to many regulations. It also experiences significant fluctuations in throughput due to incoming waste material quality variation. The potential buyers walked away from this deal, and the business eventually closed.

Beg, Borrow, or Buy

You do not have the time to reinvent the wheel.

In fact, you are required to borrow other wheels. When that is not enough, begging and buying are essential for fast, profitable growth. I assure you that **your competitors are practicing this approach all the time**. They go further by finding ways to derail your efforts and put you out of business.

No matter how brilliant you and your team are, sooner or later you will face the decision whether or not to beg, borrow, and steal an idea, product, and/or concept from others. You need to be open to the competitor's influence on your business from R&D to production, marketing, and sales. Some of the most successful companies owe their success to the founders using this approach to great effect.

Finding out how to accomplish a task, such as evaluating a product performance in R&D in a cost-effective, timely manner, is one aspect. There is just not enough time in a day to do it all by ourselves—and not miss windows of opportunity. We need to be open to learn from our competition, clients, and others. Seek input in all aspects of your business.

Once again, I suggest you leave your ego behind. You need to be out looking for ideas and solutions to challenges you are encountering in your business. **Ask and you shall be rewarded.** This effort could be as simple as looking over patents or published technology papers by your competitors. If your competitor is a publicly traded stock company, their 10K report and annual reports to shareholders are available. These documents detail their focus, revenue sources, competition, future plans, and resources. I call this tactic working smart and taking shortcuts on your path to greater success and adding value to your business. Monitor their websites at all times. We learned a lot from disclosures on our competitors' websites.

Do not forget to hire away talent from your competitors. That's a smart move.

Negotiations

Negotiations are key to your success in business—whether raising funds, hiring, selling, or dealing with suppliers. When you're selling your business, learn to negotiate well by being confident and knowing the facts about your business's future potential and the buyer's intentions.

Do not go it alone. Bring another person on your team to any negotiation event. Most scientists/engineers are not comfortable with the negotiation process. We are trained to use logic and methods to solve problems. But we are also emotionally tied to our startups. To most of us, negotiations appear as a cumbersome, uncomfortable aspect of business operations to be resolved quickly. Some founders think too highly of themselves and their inventions. These are critical mistakes. Learn about the negotiation process, have gambits at hand, and arm yourself with negotiation skills, including patience and playing the reluctant buyer role. Understand why your client and/or buyer wants to do business with you. Yes you. Do not let your ego and personality get in the way of the win-win deal. **It's not personal; it's business**.

If negotiating is not your strength, realize your limitations and hire someone to negotiate on your behalf. We did, and it worked. This approach is very cost effective because it allows you to focus on your core competency, which usually means getting back in the lab and doing what you like. You need someone who has had experience doing deals in your niche. Pay attention to the fine print. Negotiate clawback clauses to protect your interests.

As for licensing deals, you need to ensure ways to verify royalty payments on net sales and not profits (gross or not) since you have no control over their operating costs. Also set up simple, low-cost accounting ways to verify licensee honesty in reporting revenue. You need to negotiate to have solid, low-cost recourse if a licensing deal is violated or terminated.

Always have options and backup plans for any deal you are evolved in. These allow you to play the role of the reluctant buyer or seller, and at times the backup option might turn out to be a better deal.

After the deal is done, learn to renegotiate. Yes, that is correct, though it's not something we practice often. After the deal is complete, request to renegotiate if you discover you made a mistake, missed some facts, or misunderstood the contract. Events will take place that impact the deal adversely and in unexpected ways. Be prepared and willing to renegotiate. This is referred to in the agreements also as clawback clauses. Request to include them in.

Chapter 12
Working Your Contacts

Contacts are critical in every aspect of your startup—educators, consultants, mentors. I am astonished how many entrepreneurs try to work in a bubble. You need to ask for assistance and answers to your questions for various aspects of your venture. Here are some important contacts to cultivate and nurture.

Educators

Colleges and universities are good places for technical support. Student interns, research staff, and others at higher education establishments can provide support.

In my businesses, we also attended and presented at research conferences to keep up with new technology developments and to meet the key customer business success drivers.

Consultants

Retirees from your competitors' staffs make great consultants. I have always hired consultants to support our objectives. Often, they are the low-cost option to solving critical challenges.

Mentors

Seek experienced mentors and win them over. Over the years, I have been fortunate to get support, advice, guidance, and empathy from multiple mentors. I welcomed the opportunity to learn from mentors, including my college advisor and other startup CEOs. They are an important part of your contacts and advisors.

Early on in our first venture, I received advice from another CEO. I was complaining about lack of revenue—even though we had endorsements. His response was, "You are building credibility, and sales will follow. Be patient. You are on the right path." And he was right.

As I've grown older, I appreciate the support of mentors more and more. They will see you through rough patches growing your business—and there are always rough patches. Often, mentors have experience in aspects of business that you lack or do not have the time to develop. Seek out your mentors at decision times and get their advice on key decisions. Ask questions.

Chapter 13
Using Internal vs. External Production

For various reasons, some founders wish to build vertically integrated business, which means to set up your own operations, including manufacturing. I advise against it. Do not allow any activity that prevents focus on your potential customers and their feedback. If you must, keep R&D and pilot production. There are lessons to be learned during pilot production of your products that R&D lab bench tests can not reveal. Having your own full-scale production of your products takes time away from focusing on customer-driven product development. Setting up your own operations requires substantial additional resources and time. Have multiple suppliers and constantly be on the lookout for more.

In my businesses, we were fortunate in looking for and digging up backup options as material suppliers or contract manufacturers.

For our first startup, we set up in-house manufacturing operations. In our second and subsequent ventures, we outsourced manufacturing to contract manufacturers (toll blenders). While in pursuit of toll blenders for our most recent venture, thanks to an introduction by a friend, we found a toll blender in northern California. This contractor specializes in producing specialty chemical formulations like ours and sourcing raw materials. The contractor's capabilities and sourcing turned out to be major boosts to our product development. Using a toll blender for our ventures freed up our time to focus on customer needs and product development. Also, the toll blenders had better quality control programs in place than we did.

It can be argued that setting up your own in-house production can improve profit margins. One needs to do a thorough evaluation of the Return on Investment (ROI) to decide if it makes business sense. In my case, the benefits of outsourcing far outweighed any potential drop in profit margins. In one toll blending case, we actually lowered our material costs because they were buying the same raw material in much larger volumes at much lower prices than we would.

Chapter 14
Doing Research and Development

Often, a business founder's core competency comes from R&D, leading to product development. But not always. Many a business has started due to discovering unfulfilled market needs. There are times when:

- We discover a crossover of a technology from one industry segment into another.

- We find an underserved market by territory.

- We stumble upon a new application for an existing product.

- Our clients make us aware of a new product/ application need.

Many of our colleges and universities in the United States are centers of excellence in multiple science and technology fields generating numerous inventions. Many successful ventures have spun out of US-based research centers. Given the availability of venture funding in the United States, there are ample opportunities to explore entrepreneurship in commercializing risky ventures. Commercializing pioneering innovation is best carried out in the United States. The rest of the world knows this and looks for it in startups based in and funded in the US. In Palo Alto, California, I came across a venture capitalist looking for entrepreneurs. He indicated they had the funds and the business opportunities. They were looking for entrepreneurs to step up and manage the ventures.

Please note marketing is more important to your success

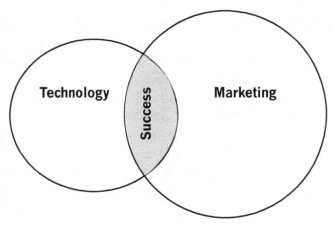

than technology, hence the larger circle for markting in the Venn diagram.

All of these discoveries are most often driven by your marketing. Marketing must decide which of these findings justifies a pivot in R&D resources and set priorities. Note that none of these findings are what the R&D team might find to be essential. Marketing drives the allocation of resources.

When is a product/service ready for commercialization? When the customer says so—not when your R&D team decides. Windows of opportunity do not linger for your R&D team to complete and perfect an offering.

Sometimes our clients made our initial offerings work by modifying their processes to meet deadlines they had to comply with. I found it necessary to have our R&D team in close contact with our clients. We had product managers who participated in the sales efforts. Product managers were a vital link between our R&D team and the customer's end users. Often the founders initially wear many hats developing and selling the products. This approach should be encouraged.

What is your offering? What is the opportunity?

How soon can you get a prototype in the hands of your potential customers? The sooner the better. You need their feedback ASAP. That is working smart.

The early adopters are the customers you need to go after. They are typically based in the United States. Their feedback is essential to your R&D, and their input and approval will expedite your success.

Are you able to get the early adopters to participate in your product development? Go for it!

Can you simply describe the benefits of your novel product/service and get the end user to agree?

Opportunities arise when there are changes in your customer's production driven by innovation and their own customers' demands.

The rate of change in technology is increasing rapidly, often making existing operations obsolete. Existing potential customers must keep up with their customers' marketplace demands. New developments in technology are providing new ways to conduct operations.

There are different approaches and methods to conduct R&D. Overlapping of sciences is a fertile ground for innovation. Mixing talented team members with different backgrounds in education and experience can often lead to surprising innovations.

Here are a few R&D options.

Newton Approximation Method

Newton's Method, also known as *Newton Raphson Method*, is important because it's an iterative process that can approximate solutions to an equation with incredible accuracy. And it's a method to approximate numerical solutions (i.e., x-intercepts, zeros, or roots) to equations that are too hard for us to solve by hand. This approach is often used to optimize performance of a product in operations.

In my graduate school days the calculator Ti-80 was used to calculate certain unknown answers in design of distillation columns, which included the 32-step Newton approximation method. Now software is used on tools to do the same online.

We see this approach applied daily to product process optimization by customers using feedback control loops. For example, maintaining the optimum performance is based on time, temperature, and concentration parameters of our products. This method uses programmable logic software. Adjustments in operating parameters are continuously being made by real time online monitoring. In one case, a client of ours tracked down poor process performance to improper dilution of our product on one of their operating tools. A dilution monitoring system was not operating properly.

Design of Experiments (DOE)

This is a systematic, efficient method that enables scientists and engineers to study the relationship between multiple input variables (aka factors) and key output variables (aka responses). It is a structured approach for collecting data and making discoveries.

In my businesses, we mostly used this approach, and it takes time. However, we would bring in customer test samples and feedback to expedite the process. We call this closing the loop to expedite R&D efforts. We were fortunate not to conduct R&D in a bubble.
At times, we cut short the optimization of the product performance and sent samples out to potential clients in order not to miss the windows of opportunity. R&D teams had to have potential clients involved in goal settings, which invariably also dictated the allowable time available to do the work.

Our R&D team used the DOE approach to conduct

research. But development required more of a Newton's approach as we worked out processing guidelines to use our product in our customers' production steps.

R&D Through Partnering

We also had to do joint product development by relying on third-party equipment vendors. Our products were evaluated in their R&D and applications labs on processing tools and analysis equipment we could not afford. This arrangement was very helpful in expediting our R&D efforts at minimum cost to us. They also contributed to our R&D with their feedback and suggestions. Our customers were also involved working with these very same OEMs in their application labs. Our potential clients were developing their new production line processes for new electronic devices, including semiconductor devices for logic and memory applications. In one case, after a demo with an OEM, two key potential accounts came calling. That was a win-win arrangement for both the OEM and us.

Customers as R&D Partners

Customers' needs for a product/technology must drive your R&D focus.

Some of our customers had substantial internal R&D resources and pilot operations tackling the same issues for which we were developing products. They worked with our team to overcome shortcomings and provide invaluable input. They were struggling with meeting specifications and deadlines imposed by their customers. We were fortunate with market timing based on the customer's immediate needs—windows of opportunity. In some cases, we were able to secure customers for our products based upon timely feedback by evaluating our products in their facilities. We were solving their immediate needs, and they did whatever they could to make our product work for them.

We were given access to their facilities, and our R&D team was able to spend time with their staff.

Blue Sky Thinking

Blue sky thinking is a form of creative thinking without boundaries, judgements, or consequences. Allow and encourage input from any member of the team without imposing your own views.

When you have an open mind, inspiration from multiple sources leads to inventions. Innovation can then take place in various aspects of the venture, including marketing, production, and R&D.

In my businesses, our student interns often had fresh ideas and inspired our R&D team to think outside the box. We also always sent meeting agendas before meetings—to get people thinking ahead of time. In meetings, make sure to state the challenge and allow everyone to brainstorm verbally or in writing at the meeting or later. This approach allows the staff to think without pressure. Often during meetings, one or two attendees tend to dominate the conversation and have a lot to say. Control the meeting, ensuring everyone can express themselves without prejudice.

During one session when we were looking for an additive for one of our formulations, we had an a-ha moment. One of the team members suggested an ingredient found as a preservative in a jam jar. That ingredient was exactly what we needed. We managed to get a patent on the formulation with this ingredient, and the product became our best seller.

The rapid introduction and growth of new semiconductor device technology and market expansions forced our customers to work closely with their suppliers, including our small businesses. The pressure our clients were under to innovate or lose their customers made them open to new ideas and products.

Chapter 15
Working with Suppliers

Nothing jeopardizes your business's value more than being single sourced to one supplier. Why? Because any interruption in supply source deliveries can kill your business. The quality of your suppliers' products and your relationships with them are critical to your success when exiting your business—just as they are while operating your business.

Whether you are buying for production and/or R&D purposes, treat your suppliers well. My motto has always been: Treat your supplier's staff—from secretary to management—as you would treat your customers.

Your suppliers can give you valuable intel on your competition. Your supplier's sales rep is a significant link to your marketplace because they are often also supplying your competitors.

Initially, to get a supplier's attention, you need to court them and win them over. Because your initial purchases will likely have small dollar values, you might not get the attention you need. Yet your supplier's reliability, logistics, and pricing can make or break your product development efforts. Hence supply chain concerns.

In my businesses, we always looked for backup options to our material suppliers and product contract manufacturers. It's critical to have multiple suppliers for each product component or service need of your business. We decided to establish 3-month inventories near our customer operations and providing Just-in-Time (JIT) service. Do the same with your suppliers.

Always be on the lookout for backup options and alternatives to how you operate now. This is when having a team is of great value to you and your business's future. You cannot grow your business without delegating and sharing responsibilities. Any company that wants to buy your business will look for this approach to ensure longevity of your business's growth potential.

Chapter 16
Securing Funding

In business, there are two types of funding needed: working capital and capital investments. Often, we must trade equity in our businesses for some funding options. We need to minimize dilution and reduction of our equity position in the business, while also ensuring we are adequately capitalized. Maintaining the majority equity position provides owners with more control of the business, and you will reap a greater reward when exiting the business.

Working capital, also referred to as operating expenses, made up of inventory, payments, day-to-day expenses, is considered short-term expenses.

Capital investments (Capital Expenditure) are substantial long-term investments.

When most businesses are founded, the owners raise funds for both working capital and capital investments. Later, as the business grows, we usually mostly need capital for large investments.

Share Classes

Most popular way to raise funds is by selling equity stock (shares) in your company. Equity ownership in the business is defined by shares. There are different types of shares, including common shares, non-voting common shares, preferred common shares, and options. Most small businesses sell common shares to raise funds. However, venture capital investors want to create and buy preferred common shares, which offer benefits, such as board seats and the right of return of capital invested.

For our first venture, rather than fund raising, we initially went without salaries, and we invested our own personal savings and took out credit cards and loans from family and friends. Early on, one angel investor purchased 1% equity (common shares) for $5,000.

For our first two ventures, we secured loans/warrants from the Ben Franklin Technology Partners of Northeastern Pennsylvania (BFTP-NEP) state program. Always look for state and local sources of capital for your business.

For my second venture, I sold two classes of stocks—voting and non-voting common shares—to raise needed funds. I kept all 1,000 voting shares for myself. This strategy allowed me to maintain full control over the business. I also kept about 60% of the non-voting stock. Thereafter, for my other startups, I used mostly my own funds as well as BFTP loans as needed.

In neither venture did we have venture capital investors. But we did get their input and guidance. Very few venture capitals invest in chemical firms. For at least the past 20 years, most investments by venture capitals is in eCommerce, software, and IT.

Save Money with Early Adopter Clients

If you want to raise less money, get your potential clients involved in your R&D. Ideally, you want your customers to sponsor and conduct some of your R&D. You will then need less funding, get valuable timely feedback, and experience rapid commercialization of your invention.

Find those risk-takers. By evaluating our products in their facilities, our potential customers saved us significant costly resource commitments. These same driven, early adopters made our products work in their operations. The customers overcame our product performance short-comings by modifying their process recipes. Having customers evaluate and purchase our products early on greatly reduced our funding needs to invest in resources and staffing.

Grants, Research Funds, and Government Assistance

You might wish to explore federal, state, and local sources of funding. It pays to look for the low-hanging fruit by doing your research and asking your contacts. These various government funding options require submission of application forms and a proposal following the provided guidelines.

In my businesses, we successfully tapped the Ben Franklin Technology Partnership (BFTP) multiple times for loans. Initially, they took a chance on us. They also provided us with lab space for our research and development efforts, which was critical. We have had four startups supported by BFTP, and we are indebted to the organization and their wonderful staff support for more than 35 years.

In Pennsylvania, the Keystone Innovation Zone (KIZ) program provides resources, including loans. In the Lehigh Valley, the Community Action Committee Lehigh Valley offers a loan program. These applications can take a while to process, and they usually award the funds in stages, but you should be sure to explore your local community for state and local support and funding.

Having unsuccessfully attempted to pursue federal funding sources such as the Small Business Innovation Research (SBIR) grants, we decided to focus on early adoptor customers. However, do not ignore federal, state, county, and local sources of funding and other forms of assistance.

Another federal financing source for small businesses option is the Small Business Administration's 7(a) Loan Program. This loan program includes financial help for small businesses with special requirements. Basic uses for this loan include establishing a new business or assisting in the acquisition, operation, or expansion of an existing business. This program is the best option when real estate is part of a business purchase, but it can also be used for:

- Short- and long-term working capital
- Refinance current business debt
- Purchase furniture, fixtures, and supplies

The maximum loan amount for a 7(a) loan is $5 million. Key eligibility factors are based on what the business does to receive its income, its credit history, and where the business operates.

The buyer of your business often finances a portion or all the financing to purchase your business through third party financing, and the buyer might well tap into this 7(a) loan.

Creativity vs. Funding

There is an inverse relation between funding and creativity.

We often hear, "If only we had more funding!" It is not so.

Access to too many funds can make the startup founders negotiate less and spend more. Funding encourages the tendency to build overhead that is not essential to the growth of the venture. You must operate mean and lean. **Stay hungry, lean, and agile—and continue to be creative**. The investors and potential buyers of your business will greatly appreciate this mode of operation.

There are multiple sources of funding. Make sure you know what the funding you are seeking is for. Do your homework, which entails preparing a business plan. Most funding sources will require a business plan, which is a roadmap that demonstrates your awareness and understanding of your technology market niche and path to rapid growth. They also need to know how you will spend the funds raised.

However, the investors look to the management maturity and experience in managing the business. Often the scientist/engineer inventor is not skilled nor interested in managing a startup. He/she would rather be in the lab, developing the next cool technology and letting others handle what he/she perceives to be the mundane aspects of the business. In such cases, lucky are the founders who recognize this weakness and team up with cofounders ASAP. Scientists/engineers typically have a low opinion of sales and marketing aspects of the business and look down on the folks involved in these functions. This is a fatal weakness. Few inventors want to invest the time to understand their customers' needs. Not many are comfortable articulating their vision to the customers and others. But initially they must.

You might be thinking, *Is it not obvious?* We take for granted that our invention is so impactful that others will instantly understand its benefits. This is not the case, especially with novel disruptive technology. Remember who pays the bills and that customers, investors, and buyers are not stupid.

Reduce Funding Needs by Reducing Overhead

Less long-term, fixed, financial commitment will appeal to your business's buyers. To make your exit plan more successful, make this an active part of your operation mode.

Minimize building up your overhead for as long as you can and reduce or minimize your fixed overhead. Outsource as much of your operation as possible. Overhead is an expensive trap that burdens many startups with unnecessary expenses and distraction. Your main goal is to get your prototype into the hands of your potential clients. All the funding and profits should go toward accomplishing that goal. Focus on sales, marketing, and rapid product development in response to customer feedback. This is what the buyer of your business values—not the brick-and-mortar investments. The buyer is looking for sustainable growth potential and profitability.

Rent equipment and space—rather than buying them. Look for business startup incubators and/or shared space to keep costs down. This approach should allow you to reduce overhead and generate significant additional net profits.

We started and operated our first venture out of my basement. When we outgrew my basement, we moved to the newly established BFTP business incubator on the campus of Lehigh University in Bethlehem, Pennsylvania.

Our second, third, and fourth companies were also set up at the BFTP business incubator. We stayed in business incubators until our business expansion forced us to move.

Another way to manage your overhead is to contract out manufacturing, accounting, legal, and any other operational aspects that you are not an expert in. Word of caution: Outsource, but remain involved. Have regular meetings with the contractors and inspect the work outsourced. Be on the lookout for backups. Large firms have teams of engineers and inspectors at their contractors' operation sites working side by side with them, supporting their efforts to optimize and improve their capabilities.

A few times, our customers visited us to inspect our production operations and contract manufacturers for quality control purposes. During one visit, a customer's engineer provided us with valuable production process suggestions, which we quickly incorporated—saving time and money while producing a more consistent product.

Venture Capital and Angel Investors

You could reach out to the many venture capital firms and angel investment groups if you are developing eCommerce, IT, software, or smart phone apps. But very few venture capital firms invest in hardware and other tangible products. An annual review conducted by the San Jose *Mercury* newspaper found that less than 5% of all capital venture investments was in tangible, hardware-based companies.

There are many individual angel investors—like me. There are now also more institutional capital venture divisions within large fortune 1000 companies.

If for no other reason, approaching, meeting, and submitting a business plan to a few select venture capital firms is of great value because these firms are managed by bright, experienced folks who can provide valuable feedback on your business. They also have lots of contacts.

If you are turned down by venture capital firms, do not be insulted, depressed, or upset. They have their niche focus. Even though they review thousands of business plans, they typically invest in only a few each year. Even so, their investment record shows at best only 1 out of 10 companies they invest in has a successful exit. So, they are very selective in the choice of companies in which they invest. They can also be quite demanding in the percentage of business startup ownership they wish to own. They will also insist on having members of their team on your board. They are great at negotiating, too.

Our first business was turned down by the only local venture fund we approached—for good reason. But having them review our business plan and receiving their feedback was instrumental to our future success. Given their input and recommendations, I ended up as the president of our first venture, and we focused on one niche market—rather than shot-gunning the markets as we had been doing. Our original 100-page business plan was shrunk to 20-pages, which attests to the value of input.

We see more and more large corporations in more traditional manufacturing industries also setting up their venture capital division. For example, the American Institute of Chemical Engineers has an annual venture conference where startups can pitch their businesses. Large chemical firms and others in this industry attend. My concern, which might be unfounded, is pitching your business vision/product and niche too early to the outside world without any confidentiality agreements. Any information that's presented at these events is considered public information, including your valuable data. Stop broadcasting your niche, vision, and product to the whole world. That is not operating in stealth mode. You are tipping off your competitors.

Instead, hold confidential meetings with qualified, screened investors. There you can control the disclosure of information and execute NDAs to ensure your info disclosed is kept confidential.

Even if your technology is well protected by patents, do not initially openly promote your technology—not even on your own website. At times, I see startups disclosing far too much information online about their niche focus and technology.

Other Sources of Funding

Another way to "fund" is by spending less money! The more you save, the less you need to raise funds and the less you dilute your equity by holding onto more of your business shares. The less equity you need to give up will provide you with more control over your vision and your business management.

Get your suppliers, consultants including attorneys, and manufacturer's reps (selling your products) to agree to favorable terms. Barter with them. Invite them to invest in your business.

We did, and it paid off well for all involved. We also negotiated favorable terms with suppliers, contract manufacturers, and other investors in direct and indirect funding of our startups.

We realized significant savings from in-kind support from other vendors selling to our mutual customers. We were able to minimize our investments in R&D and pilot equipment by cooperating with other suppliers to our mutual potential customers.

Bank Financing

Finally, it is worth mentioning that banks are not in the business of investing in startups. Banks will not take the risk. However, once you have generated revenue and developed credit, you can tap the following two worthwhile banking services.

Factoring: This is early payment by the bank for a fee against your invoices to your customers for products/service delivered. We did not use this service.

Line of credit: As you grow your business and generate significant revenue, banks are willing to provide you with lines of credit. In the early stages of your venture, banks might lend your company money, but they will invariably require personal guarantees against your personal assets as collateral. We did take advantage of this service often.

Chapter 17
Understanding the Impact of Patents

In business, patents are both a blessing and a distraction. In most acquisitions, the buyer is interested in and values the patents protecting your technology. Holding patents carves out a space that provides you with market share exclusivity. Patents are the government's way of supporting your small business based on your technology, innovation, and novelty.

But know that patents are offensive weapons—not defensive weapons. Patent infringement has been used to stop copycats and defend one's market position. However, litigations are very expensive, time-consuming, and emotionally taxing.

Competitors' patents are a great source of information on your niche and your competitors. The US government patent office provides online access to all issued US patents.

When working on your exit plan, keep in mind that organizations that own related patents might be candidates that would be interested in purchasing your business.

In all our ventures, we pursued obtaining patents. Beginning in 1995, we used the Provisional Patent Application (PPA) option. The PPA option is a gift to small businesses and startups because it provides you with the unique opportunity to claim patent pending technology from the date you submit your simple, brief, low-cost PPA to the US patent office. A PPA gives you 12 months to complete and submit a full patent. It gives you an official filing date, although your application does not get reviewed or published.

Overall, if not for the value placed on patents by business buyers, I am not sure how much of company resources should be allocated to securing patents—instead of focusing on sales and securing market share. There needs to be a balance. Provisional patents provide the marketing team with the opportunity to promote the new product and decide whether securing a patent is worthwhile.

In my businesses, only about 2 out of 10 product patents (80/20 rule) we secured were commercial successes. However, we did use 1 patent in federal court to settle and force a licensee to stop producing and selling one of our products.

We decided to abandon our growing third venture based on patent infringement allegations and litigations by a competitor. The management of a competing division of very large, stock-traded, multidivisional company was out to get us. They claimed patent infringement and forced us out of business—given the cost of litigations. Even though we won the first few rounds in the United States and South Korea patent office litigations, the company continued to appeal and bleed us with the high legal fees necessary to defend our positions. Under advice from our attorney, we gave up. Our competitor refused to allow us a license, which they had initially promised.

Chapter 18
Pivoting

As you operate your business, mindful of your eventual exit, you must be open to pivot. In fact, most potential buyers of your business will respect your ability to pivot and consider that as valuable experience when they evaluate your company.

As 13th-century Persian poet and mystic Rumi said: "Yesterday, I was clever, so I wanted to change the world. Today, I am wise, so I am changing myself."

To pivot is to change direction to survive and thrive. I do not know of any successful business that has not pivoted. You do not have to be the ship's captain who stays on and goes down with the sinking ship. Pivoting is smart. You owe it to your crew—and to yourself.

In various aspects of your venture, including your market focus and R&D, you probably will need to pivot your approach/focus and choose different options as you gain experience and obtain feedback. Often your business's initial product/service commercialized will not be the product that will generate significant revenue. Your product will go through iterations (like the Newton Approximation Method—see page 85) as you collect performance data from end users of your technology. More than 60% of businesses funded by venture capitalists pivot their market focus, too. You might be pleasantly surprised to find other applications or opportunities for your products and expertise.

In our first venture, we pivoted three times, from consulting on environmental regulations to product development for semiconductor device fabrication industry as well as the agricultural insect control niche. We dropped the agricultural insect control product soon after its market introduction. In the semiconductor fabrication niche, we had a few products for three different applications. We dropped all but one.

Failing is an option, as long as you learn from it, pivot, and move on.

There will be unanticipated roadblocks. Consider that even airline flight routes are adjusted to account for turbulence and traffic. Today when we drive, we use the navigation systems in our smart phones or cars. When we select a destination, we are given alternative routes to get there. On the way, we are warned of traffic jams and offered alternative routes. Pivoting on an ongoing basis is part of our lives, which allows us to work smart, minimize effort, save time, and reduce waste.

To pivot is to thrive. It is not admission of failure. Successful salespersons are great at pivoting during the sales efforts. It's part of their sales strategy to constantly look for feedback and customers' signals when presenting the benefits of their product/service. Often during my presentations to customers, I have altered my presentation sequence and focus to respond to my audience's feedback.

Chapter 19
Supporting Your Team

Few things are more important as you grow your business than the people you add to your team. The company staff will be critical to your success, and they will also be important to how you exit your business.

Investors and companies looking to buy small businesses are looking for talented people in various divisions of the business, including R&D, sales and marketing, and operations. Having the right people in these positions will add value to your business.

Build a team that can help you continue to grow the business rapidly. The acquirer of your company looks for depth of management that can run the business without you needing to micromanage the business.

Your venture is going to be built on hiring smart dedicated team members who are committed and believe in the business mission. Agility is your main advantage over larger competitors. You can take advantage of your agility mostly by delegating.

In the beginning, you probably hire all team members yourself. But as your business grows, this is an important task to delegate. Typically, the inventor and other cofounders need assistance with all human resources aspects of the business like this. It takes time to find qualified, experienced staff who will enhance the capabilities needed to succeed.

As I've mentioned: Beg or borrow talent—especially from your competitors. Their loss is your gain.

Once you find and hire great team members, you want to keep them! Motivating and keeping staff is critical. Acknowledge and reward good performance. Celebrate outstanding achievements. Nothing motivates your team more than recognition of great performance by individual team members. This practice will also boost morale—inexpensively.

Do not micromanage your team. You will exhaust yourself and slow the process of developing your staff.

Allow for and encourage innovation in various aspects of the venture by encouraging the staff to provide ideas and suggestions. (Make this part of the culture.) Learn to LISTEN to the whole team. (But do not be the in-house counselor, or you will be spending a lot of time listening to staff grievances.)

Hire and partner with team members who are smarter than you. Leave your ego behind. They know you are the boss.

Remember to work smart—not just hard. As your company grows, delegate as much as you can to your team and staff, especially routine activities. This allows you to focus on strategy and adding value to your business.

Also, delegating will allow you to take time off, relax, spend more time with your family, and be creative. Your business must be able to function *without* your daily input and direction. That is a significant way of adding value to your business in preparation for your exit.

Work yourself out of your job.

Job Titles

In many companies, job titles are everything. Let the large firms use these titles and have their employees fight over them.

In my businesses, we didn't put job titles on our business cards, to take away the internal politicking for titles. The

Return on Investment (ROI) for this action was remarkable. There were no coveted titles to aim for and fight over in our businesses. It was one less point of contention.

A reminder: A company officially (legally) has three officers: president, secretary, and treasurer. In my opinion, all other titles are unnecessary. They can often lead to resentment and infighting among the staff.

As for having relatives work at the company, I am not sure it is a great idea. Anything that is impacted by emotions involved due to relationships at work can and must be checked early on. Unfortunately, we learned this lesson the hard way. In our first venture, we had a rough time adjusting and coping with having relatives work together in the business. It made decision-making difficult because business success is all about business and not personal—unless we make it personal.

Do not live with your mistakes. If a staff member is not a team player or slows down or disrupts your growth, let him/her go sooner than later. Your team will appreciate this and look to your leadership and respect that you will not tolerate poor performance and disruptions of the venture.

No one is indispensable. If you think a person is indispensable, your business will suffer because you tend to give in under threat of those founders or key employees leaving the business. That's not good for business. Fortunately, in a small business, the staff wears many hats, and there is plenty of overlap in duties and responsibilities. So let them leave if they cannot be team players or get rid of them. Over the past five businesses I owned and operated, fortunately I only had to let go three team members.

We were fortunate to have hired many talented scientists and engineers who believed in our vision—and a few who did not. As founders, we are role models. You must motivate and manage the team. Look out for internal friction among the employees and resolve it ASAP. We let go of a few people who we could neither train nor motivate to be team players.

In our second business, we made all the staff, as well as a few consultants, shareholders by offering them stock options. We also insisted that the purchaser of that business retain our staff and a number of our international sales representatives. We had more than 30 shareholder signatures on the business purchase agreement. Many stayed on and ended up in key positions in our former business which become a division of the buyer's organization.

We had pension funds, health insurance, and other perks for our staff. We gave bonuses and Christmas gifts. We included the staff in most decision-making. Often, we found suggestions and feedback from our team to be a significant source of ideas for doing things better. During R&D meetings, we had sales staff, product managers, and manufacturing folks take part and contribute.

The staff directly involved in dealing with and selling to your customers—especially your sales team and tech support—are especially important members of your team. Train and treat them well and keep them motivated. Initially, founders are often the most effective salespeople to be selling and promoting the venture's products given their understanding and passion for the technology.

One last important note about your team: I want to emphasize the importance of marketing and arts as being equal to science and technology. I like collaboration and communication of these various disciplines. You will find lots of innovation where there is overlap of disciplines.

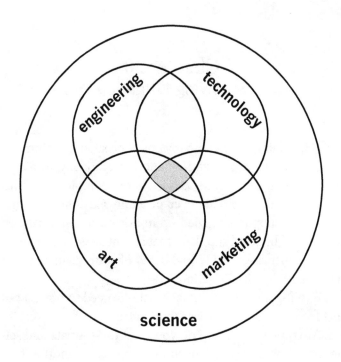

Chapter 20
Surviving Litigation

Sooner or later, your company could be sued or you might need to sue someone and/or another company to assure your business's future. My advice here is simple. **Avoid litigation at all costs whenever possible**. Customers do not want their suppliers tangled up in litigation. Potential customers might avoid suppliers that are involved in litigation. And in most cases a potential buyer of your business wants nothing to do with litigation.

But litigation is a necessary evil. We need to protect our turf from invaders, copycats, and outright theft.

Anytime issues arise, do your best to negotiate and settle, even if you are challenged by a copycat or another firm claiming you infringe on their patents. My advice is to get engaged in talks early. Start negotiating ASAP. Negotiations allow you to befriend the other company and to see their points of view, the merits of their case, and what will satisfy them. Do not ignore the threat. My experience is that, against all odds, licensing technology involved could lead to possible future partnerships.

Do your best to settle ASAP. Litigating is expensive, time-consuming, and emotionally draining. We sued and were sued on three separate occasions. In Appendix D, you can read about a few cases we were involved in.

Chapter 21
Other Key Topics

Here are some more important issues to consider while growing—and then exiting—your business.

Small Business Ombudsman

Small Business Ombudsman is a federal agency that supports, protects, and assists small businesses against over-zealous government agency staff actions. This is one of few federal government programs that we partook and highly recommend. Not many founders and small business management staff are aware of nor tap this valuable resource until it's too late.

Early in our second business, this organization rescued us from Federal Aviation Agency (FAA) fines. We were fined $750,000 for 35 FAA violations due to improper paperwork filings! Just as our venture was about to take off. We managed to settle this case with the support of the small business ombudsman for $3,500. And we went on to grow a successful business in 5 years with more than 30 employees.

I believe that this great federal organization's efforts should also be expanded to include protection of startups from large competitors. That would be good for the economy—and for consumers. Let the best products that save time and money flourish—no matter what size business owns the technology. Most of the time it's small businesses that take the most risk and innovate.

Entrepreneurs are risk takers and innovators. Most people don't realize that small businesses have more employees in total than the Fortune 1000 companies combined.

Unfortunately, our federal and state governments at times may allow large competitors to use any method to block, derail, and even destroy their small startup competitors. This is where conniving practice may rise its ugly head again. Small businesses provide more jobs, but large companies have the corporate clout, deep pockets, and lobbying power in Washington, DC.

Advertising, Trade Shows, and Conferences

It is easy to spend a fortune on advertising to try to keep up with your competitors. Do not.

Instead, use your contacts, word of mouth, and public relations to get your name and product out there. Do not advertise too early. Stay low and work in stealth mode as long as you can. Typically, in technology-based niches there are only a select number of potential customers. There is no need for mass advertising. Save your money. Invest in experienced, connected sales representatives instead. Advertising is an expensive trap and a distraction. In this day and age, a well-designed, informative website will suffice. Your customers want data backed by demonstrations and validation by third party entities—not flashy ads.

Attend trade shows as well as R&D conferences. Both are excellent sources of contacts and are the place to reach key decision makers. I have found attending conferences and exhibits associated with the industry niche to be fertile grounds for looking for business and learning about competition.

But don't spend money to have your own booth at the shows. After having had our own exhibit booths a few times, we decided that we were better off saving the time and money that goes in to setting up and staffing the booth by just attending the conferences and exhibits.

Generate interest and credibility by publishing research papers on the performance of your products. Team up to generate data with third-party participants. Ultimately performance data generated by customers is the most valuable for your product R&D and to attract other customers. This is a form of branding your technology.

Referrals are key to your success. Having a customer endorse your technology is the ultimate, most effective form of advertising.

Exporting

Export your product/technology to grow your business and outmaneuver your competition.

First establish your product performance, packaging needs, logistics, and processing needs by securing a few local customer accounts. You should then look for select exporting opportunities.

We had the good fortune to successfully export our products for our various startup ventures. More than 50% of our sales were generated in Asia and Europe. We followed on the coattails of our US-based customers and competitors to accounts in South Korea, Japan, Taiwan, and Singapore in Asia. In Europe, we sold to companies in France, Italy, and more. We found manufacturer's representatives and distributors to sell for us in Asia and Europe. The best way to find international agents was through other US companies exporting contacts or US-based sales agencies. These international sales agents were of great assistance in sales and marketing of our products, including pricing for our international customers. In one case, we were able to raise prices for a client of ours prior to offering them our price list and negotiating. That was based on feedback and suggestions by a sales rep in Taiwan.

We learned to understand and respect the many cultural differences in conducting business. Fortunately, the language of science is English.

Asian clients have high regard for American innovation and pioneering technology.

We were fortunate to initially sell our products to US-based customers who provided us with valuable early feedback. The US-based semiconductor fabrication companies had the R&D and pilot lines to evaluate and adopt new processing technologies. We had the opportunity to learn the necessary knowhow regarding how our product was used. We therefore were successful promoting our products overseas and generated more than half of our business through exporting.

Federal organizations like the US Commerce Services (USCS) are available to assist and support exporting efforts. I know of a few firms that successfully engaged USCS services. There are also state and local agencies that can assist. Depending on your exporting plans, these organizations can expedite the processes and be a productive resource.

Based on data available, only 10% of US GDP was based on export revenue in 2019!! In England, it was 25% and 50% for Germany. So, chances are your US competitors are ignoring the export market, or they are focused only on a few selective countries. That is a strategic marketing opportunity for your business.

Quality Control

When it comes to quality, never cut corners. Get it right the first time. When you deliver your product, it must perform as expected. It needs to meet and exceed customer quality requirements every time. It is hard for any business to recover from customers rejecting your product due to poor quality.

Set up and implement an ISO 9001 Quality Control Program. Established more than 30 years ago, ISO 9001 requires the organization to have detailed job descriptions for each employee. They need to be detailed enough so another person can take over the position without interrupting the business operations. I am glad we adopted ISO9001 and got certified. The ISO 9001 program was useful to the exit plan adoption and implementation. The buyers of your company will appreciate the professionalism required to establish the organization and staffing of the business.

We had some quality problems caused by our own or contract manufacturers. Here are a few examples.

In one case, we got a call from the quality control team of a major account telling us that their in-house composition analysis of our product showed some change. We subsequently discovered that our contract manufacturer had changed the composition of our product specs without getting our approval. Our quality control checks had not caught the change. Quite embarrassing. The good news was the change was well within the upper and lower control limits we had negotiated and set with the client. We managed to put that credibility fire out because we were prepared, and it did not hurt our business. We took quality control seriously.

In another incident, a supplier of bottle caps had changed the resin used in the caps, and they failed. We had shipped 4,000 gallons of product in 5-gallon containers to South Korea for a large client of ours—only to find out that many of the caps failed and leaked. The supplier of the caps took full responsibility, and again we averted a major upset to our business. The cap supplier did not follow protocol to first notify and allow us to qualify the new cap resin for compatibility with our product. The new cap resin was not compatible with our chemical product.

New Product Design and Introduction

Your business is continuously conducting research and development to come up with better products. You need to continue this effort based on customer feedback. However, make sure everyone on your team is on board, agrees upon, and is trained on how to respond to the changes made and new products introduced.

When I was working as VP of Sales in Asia for a tool company, I experienced firsthand what happens if you introduce too many changes too quickly. Products would be delivered to clients, and the install and service staff would be surprised by design changes, which are typically shown in red touch-ups on the product drawings. The staff on the ground struggled to install and maintain these products and the uptime of the product suffered. Many repeat orders were cancelled due to this problem.

Crisis Management

Your business is defined by how well you respond to crises.

When your business is growing, there are always crises. The startup does not just face crises; it is *defined* by them. How well you respond to a crisis ensures your success. It did for my ventures.

Always be thinking of alternative options. In addition to the previously mentioned FAA fine crisis, here are a few examples of crises we faced.

One morning, we were informed that our very first large potential account had run out of our product evaluation samples. The next morning at 8 am, they needed to process and produce more of their products using our product in their operation in Dallas, Texas. Their finished product was scheduled to ship to their new client for final qualification. We managed to get the samples air shipped and delivered by 8 pm the same day to their operation. They met the deadline and won the account. So did we.

Another time, a customer evaluating our product rejected it initially based on Environmental, Safety & Health (ES&H) regulations.

It turned out a component of our formulation concentration exceeded their internal, self-imposed ES&H

upper limit. The product had performed well in the customer evaluation. We needed a quick response to keep the qualification of our product alive. Our team came up with a creative idea that saved the account and made us more profitable! We figured out we could ship our product more diluted because the client used our product diluted. We offered the product diluted 1:1 with water and renamed the product. The client ES&H approved, and the engineers in charge of using the product signed off on it. We won the account while doubling our sales and reducing our material costs by 50%.

Setbacks remind me of the board game Chutes and Ladders. As long as you keep playing the game, you'll overcome setbacks and take advantage of the lucky breaks.

You never know when you get lucky and when setbacks strike the business. You need to play the game, persist, take the risks, deal with the setbacks, and show GRIT.

Creativity, persistence and grit are required to succeed.

Chapter 22
Life After Selling Your Business

Once you have sold your business, you are going to get calls from Wall Street types and private banking firms offering their services. You might also get calls and invites to join country clubs. Friends and relatives you did not know you had will call. They all have plans for your windfall.

Do not rush to spend the money you just made. It's almost like winning the lottery. Take a long vacation to unwind and think through your priorities in life. Plan ahead on how to invest your new-found wealth. You should have developed a plan working with your personal financial planner. Do not spoil your kids. If it's too late and you already spoiled them, at least now you can afford to pay for quality private counseling.

For some of us, it is easier to make money than to spend it.

What will you do after you sell your business? More than half of us go on to start another venture. Few successfully pivot and start new careers. I envy them. Others become employees of the buyer. Some retire.

As Buyer Employee
Get ready for culture shock.

Most founders with employment contracts often do not stay for the full term. Some might even bail out soon after the deal is consummated. The culture shock working for a large firm drives most entrepreneurs crazy. The very fact that we are not in control is enough for some to quit. Most founders find it is almost impossible to be confined by large company policies, procedures, and diversions from your interests. So, plan accordingly when you negotiate your employment agreement and company purchase agreement earn-out terms.

Typically, when you become an employee of the buyer, you will be required to sign a non-compete arrangement and an employment contract with the buyer company for a few years. (See Appendix B for excerpts and key sections from actual redacted employment agreements.)

Fight to maintain as much control over your business as possible after it is sold, especially Profit & Loss (P&L) responsibility.

Make sure you report to the CEO or someone you know has your best interest at heart. As a minimum, you should continue to be the head of your business after the acquisition, maintaining management of your operations. Insist on this provision until your business is fully integrated into the buyer's organization, which might take 6 months to 2 years. Typical employment contracts for the founders are 2 to 5 years.

Once my first business acquisition deal was done, I was made aware of certain last-minute decisions made in secret. For the deal to go through, the buyer's vice president in charge of the deal had to appease one of my former cofounders. That action regretfully impacted my role, performance, and experience at the buyer's company. The ink had not even dried on the deal when I was made to face the fact that I was to report to my unhappy, frustrated, former partner. Fortunately, our business continued to grow, meet, and exceed the earn-out goals within 2 years. I left soon after.

After Leaving the Organization

Once you leave on friendly terms and based on mutual agreement hopefully, you need to be cognizant of the various agreement's stipulations, such as non-compete, confidentiality, final payouts, and earn-out impact. Your employment contract and stock purchase agreements have several terms and conditions that impact your compensation. How and when you leave can have significant financial impact. The business purchase agreement and employment contract need to address these issues.

The employment agreements I had after the sale of my two ventures were very different in terms and conditions. When I reviewed these agreements recently, I was reminded how important it is for us to fully understand the ramification of the terms set and how they can impact your career and finances after you leave. (See Appendix B for some excerpts on two actual employment agreements.)

Newly unemployed, you now must decide what to do with yourself. After I sold my first business, as a serial entrepreneur the choice was obvious to me. I waited out the non-compete term when I left the buyer's company. I knew my industry, semiconductor fabrication niche, had contacts and friends there, and was aware of the up-and-coming changes in the customer's operations. Change in industry presents the opportunity for introducing a new product. I joined the business of a friend as their Asian market VP of sales for two years before starting my second venture.

For my second business acquisition deal, the buyer's management agreed to allow me to leave early. The non-compete restriction was waived, and they were interested in taking an equity position in my third venture. What a difference that made between the two business exits. However, after the second deal, I felt one of the buyer's executive management team members was uncooperative. He had objected to many of my decisions and plans while in their employment.

Before leaving the second buyer company, I had already

discussed and obtained their approval to start my third venture. They approved it, and they also wanted to acquire a minority (19%) equity position for a significant investment of $2 million. But they insisted on having the first right of refusal for any product my new venture would develop. Ultimately, we could not come to terms. In retrospect, I should have made the deal.

Immediately after the sale of our first business, I ran into a number of issues while serving the employment agreement. Therefore, when I found out the vice president of the buyer's business who had managed the deal was leaving, I arranged to leave too. There were a number of issues raised by the buyer's staff that were mostly instigated by a former unhappy partner in our first business. I had to resort to legal assistance to get the remaining, delayed, earn-out payments.

Also, they withheld my earn-out payment in order to enforce the non-compete term and expand the duration term to include a new process application I had discovered. I had to hire a lawyer again to fight this challenge. They backed off. I did not know they had already licensed a product from another firm for the very same application!

Interestingly, the business purchase agreement had a clause that stipulated if any of the principals left prior to the end of the employment agreement, we would forfeit the earn-out due. The earn-out according to the purchase agreement was then supposed to be distributed among the remaining principals and the buyer. However, the VP of business arranged for me to receive 85% of the earn-out. I questioned this action was not in compliance with the purchase agreement contract. His final parting comment was he will take care of that, and he did. He basically rewrote that part of the employment agreement.

Conclusion

Who is the book for again? It's for all the brave tech entrepreneurs who sooner or later will be faced with exiting their businesses for various reasons. You owe it to yourself to max out on the value of the business when you exit. You earned it. I hope that my book has offered you hardworking entrepreneurs some lessons to land win-win deals as you grow and exit your ventures.

It's best to think through the exit option and plan for this eventuality early on and structure the business as such, which requires minimizing the fixed costs of doing business vs. variable costs that can be more readily eliminated. The business must also be able to survive the departure of founders and thrive.

Occasionally, I am reminded by my previous team members how grateful they are with how well they made out from exiting our businesses. One used his portion of the buyout proceedings to pay off his mortgage. Another used his as a down payment for a new home. Some have retired, and others continue in their distinguished careers.

I've heard from consultants, investors, and others who agreed to barter their fees and invested for equity in my ventures. They thought that was a wonderful return on investment for them. The buyout of my second venture returned 10 times on the equity investments in less than 5 years.

Looking back, I realize I am a problem solver and a serial entrepreneur. I am also impatient. I lose interest once a challenge is met and overcome. I was diagnosed as having ADHD.

For me, the thrill is in discovering a market opportunity and finding the potential solution to meet the need. Then comes getting the new venture past the valley of death. That's exciting, too. Scale up and commercialization is next. Soon after, I tend to lose interest and move on to discovering the next market opportunity. And then the exit is my way to monetize my efforts.

I have been referred to as a Renaissance man, a visionary, and a serial entrepreneur. I can live with these accolades, considering other labels. Thank you. But I am not done. I am driven by solving problems, and I'm addicted to creativity. I still have a few other product ideas of my own to work on.

I am thrilled to read about and acknowledge the genius in inventors in any field, such as science, music, arts, and even military campaigns. I am amazed by the script writers' inventiveness for shows on TV or stage and the lyrics written by musicians. Listening to Mozart's music, Beatles' lyrics, and Led Zeppelin's instrumentals inspires me.

Human creativity has no boundaries.

Creating a solution for an existing problem, answering the call of a market looking for a product, and discovering novel products with disruptive impact are energizing. They are fuel for the soul.

Appendix A
Ben Franklin Technology Partners Venture Profile

The Ben Franklin Technology Partners (BFTP) offers this helpful venture profile, which you can use to capture important info on your company.

See the BFTP website for an example of a completed, fictitious venture profile.

We completed four of these venture profiles over the years and went through the required interviews. We were successful each time. We managed to secure office and lab space as well as loans from the BFTP Northeastern region, varying from $75,000 to $350,000.

- Venture concept: Describe concept and commercialization strategy.

- Background: What led to the creation of the company?

- Company team: List the founders, key members, and their roles.

- Technology: What are the key benefits of the technology?

- Targeted markets: Describe the niche market and the market segment.

- Competition: List both direct and indirect competitors.

- Product line: Explain the what, where, when, who, and how of the product.

- Commercialization: How will you reach the end users?

- Forecast (actual and 5-year forecast revenue/expenses): How much has been spent and any sales revenue? What is projected?

- Achievements to date: Do you have a prototype? What milestones have been met?

- Founder funding to date: How much have the founders invested of their own funds?

- Non-founder funding to date: Who else has invested and how much?

- Financial requirements and deal structure: How much do you need, when, and for what? For how much equity and payback?

- Plan for investor exit: Describe when and how you intend to exit and pay off the investors.

- Uses of financial proceeds: How and what will the funds be used for?

- Outside advisors: List the names and firms you are working with.

Appendix B
Stock Purchase Agreement Excerpts

Example 1- Purchase Price and Procedure for Payment

- Purchase price shall be $6,127,658 plus additional payments up to $1,400,000 as provided in section ....

- At closing Buyer shall deliver by wire transfer 70% of initial payment and hold 30% in escrow.

- Buyer will make the following additional payments:

(i) After one year- $400,000 if the contribution is between $4,600,000 and $4,750,000, or $700,000 if the contribution is $4,750,000 or more.

(ii) 2 years later- $700,000 "contribution" means gross aggregate amounts invoiced for sales of seller products for designated annual periods following closing, less (freight, ...

Example 2- Purchase Of Securities; Consideration; Closing

2.2 Consideration. (a) The aggregate purchase price for the securities (the Purchase Price") shall be the greatest of (1) $18,000,000; (2) 152.5% of the Net Revenues as calculated by the Purchaser for calendar year 2003; (3) 158.75% of the Net Revenues as calculated by Purchaser for year 2004; (4) 165% of the Net Revenues for calendar year 2005; Provided that the purchase Price shall not exceed $45,000,000.

Escrow. Purchaser shall deliver 80% of the purchase price to seller and 20% will be deposited in an Escrow Account

Note, how both deals had capped the maximum purchase price including the earn-out total. **Negotiate to remove or raise the cap on the total business purchase price.**

Actual Employment Agreement Examples Key sections for Cofounders

Example 1- Five year employment agreement

A- Employee will work for five years commencing with the closing date for the business of the acquired company.

B- Employee will receive annual salary of $115,000. Bi-weekly

C- Employer will pay employee performance bonus according to a bonus schedule

D- Employer may terminate this agreement for cause. With 30 days notice.

E- Non-compete for a period of two years after employee is no longer an employee of the buyer or for five years after the closing date of the business purchase, whichever period shall terminate later. In consideration, buyer will pay employee as follows:

Anniversary	Payment
1	$333,333
2	$266,666
3	$ 33,333
4	$ 16,666
5	$ 16,666

F- Any and all inventions, improvements, discoveries and ideas shall be the sole and exclusive of employer.

G- **Performance Bonus**

	Fiscal Year 1	Fiscal Year 2
Net Sales	16,293,081	22,000,000
Material Cost of Goods	6,221,380	8,800,000
Contribution (Gross) Margin	10,071,701	$13,200,000
Less Target	5,800,000	6,400,000
Excess over target	4,271,701	6,800,000

Bonus Rate	20%	20%
	———————	———————
Bonus Pool	854,340.20	1,360,000
Co-Founder's 1/3 share	284,780.07	453,333.33

(yes there were 3 co-founders left when we exited the first startup, we had started with four)

Example 2- Two year employment agreement for the Founder

A- The employee will serve as Director of the startup purchased with duties set forth on Schedule 1. Or in such other capacity as shall be mutually agreed by the employee and either the Board of Directors of employer or the executive management team of the employer.

B- The location of employment be within 25 miles of employee's residence or such other place as you and employer shall mutually agree.

C- Term of Employment shall terminate 2 years commencing the closing date of the acquisition. After two years your employment, unless otherwise mutually agreed upon, shall continue "at will", subject to the employer's obligation to pay the Severance Payment as provided.

D- The employer shall have the right to terminate your employment:

(a) immediately for cause

(b) Subject to section …., at any time without cause or

(c) in the event of your disability which…….

E- Employee shall have the right to terminate his employment if you "resign for just cause" which means a resignation of your employment as direct result of

(a) a material breach by the company of the obligations……

(b) a significant decrease by the Board of Directors of your duties or authority.

(c) Employer CEO ceasing to have any relationship or affiliation with the employer, provided that you have exercised such right to terminate your employment within four months of the CEO cessation of such relationship and affiliation.

(d) In the event of termination of your employment by the employer the employer shall pay to you an aggregate of six moths Base salary at the time of termination, less taxes and withholding.

F- Compensation. The company shall pay the employee a base salary at annual rate of $200,000.

G- Other benefits.

(a) Four weeks of vacation

(b) Provide you with all other employee benefits available to employees of the employer.

(c) Eligible to receive additional compensation, including awards of performance bonuses up to 100% of the base salary and grants of employee stock options, in each case in the discretion of the compensation committee of the Board of Directors of employer (which I did not receive even though the purchased business exceeded all goals and objectives in performance).

H- Non compete clause for two and half years.

You should seek advice from a licensed attorney before using or relying on this book. Additionally, none of the examples and opinions provided constitute tax advice. By using and relying on this book, you assume all risk and liability that may result.

Appendix C
Licensing and Technology Development Agreement Example

Provided below are some sections of the above agreement.

Financial sections.

License Grant and Development Fees

3.1 In consideration for the exclusive engagement provisions of Section 4.1 and the license grant defined in Sections 3.3 and 3.4, Licensee shall pay to Licensor US$100,000 within ten (10) calendar days of the Effective Date.

3.2 Subject to the early termination provisions of Section 7, Licensee shall pay to Licensor (ii) US$60,000 on each of the following dates _____, 2012; _____, 2012; _____, 2013; and _____, 2013. Such quarterly payments shall continue for any Renewal Term. Fifty (50) percent of the quarterly payments under this Section 3.2 (as listed above) made by Licensee shall be creditable by Licensee against possible royalties and exclusivity minimums under Sections 3.3 through 3.8 (below).

3.3 Provided that Licensee complies with its material obligations set forth under this Agreement, Licensor hereby grants to Licensee and Licensee Affiliates an irrevocable, royalty-bearing, worldwide, license (with the right to grant sub-licenses) under the Licensor Background Intellectual Property and the Foreground Intellectual Property in the Electronic Cleans Field to make, have made, use, sell, import, export or otherwise transfer and offer to sell Licensed Products.

3.4 (a) The license grant defined in Section 3.3 (above)

shall be (i) exclusive to Licensee as to any Target Product of the Development Program resulting from Foreground IP, (ii) exclusive to Licensee in the IC Licensor Field as to any Licensed Products, (iii) exclusive to Licensee in the Licensor Cleans Field as to Licensed Products resulting from Foreground Intellectual Property, and (iv) otherwise non-exclusive. As used in this Section 3.4, Licensee includes Licensee Affiliates.

(b) Notwithstanding the license terms specified in Section 3.3 and 3.4(a), the license grant to Licensee shall not include Licensor Existing Formulations for use outside of the Licensor Cleans Field.

3.5 For sale of Licensed Products covered by an exclusive license, Licensee shall pay to Licensor a royalty on the Net Sales of Licensed Products at a rate according to the specifications of Appendix C – Royalty Rate Calculation. For sale of Licensed Products covered by a non-exclusive license, Licensee shall pay to Licensor a royalty on the Net Sales of Licensed Products at a royalty rate of 3%.

3.6 In the event of Licensee's first commercial sale of a Licensed Product, Licensee shall pay Licensor all royalties owed within forty-five (45) days after the end of each calendar quarter. Should Licensee sales of a Licensed Product be discontinued, Licensee shall so notify Licensor . No royalty shall apply to samples of Licensed Products (i) consumed by Licensee or a Licensee contractor for testing purposes or (ii) reasonable product volumes provided to prospective customers for qualification or marketing purposes.

3.7 Should royalty payments become due as provided in Section 3.6, Licensee shall at substantially the same time then provide a royalty report to Licensor in a customary format. Licensee shall keep records in accordance with generally accepted accounting principles and in sufficient detail to permit the determination of the royalty rate calculation and royalties due to Licensor hereunder. Such records shall be kept for five (5) years following the submission of each related report. To ensure compliance with the terms and conditions of this Agreement, Licensor shall have the right to audit all relevant accounting, technical and sales books and records of Licensee, as determined in good-faith by Licensee, according to the following procedures and limitations. Upon written notice for an audit of at least forty-five (45) days in advance, Licensee shall permit a mutually acceptable independent audit firm to examine, during ordinary business hours at an office where such records are normally maintained in such a manner as not to interfere with Licensee's normal business, only records and materials of Licensee necessary for the purpose of verifying royalty computations under this Agreement. The audit report provided to Licensor may only include the information necessary to determine whether or not any underpayment or overpayment exists, and if it exists, the amount of such underpayment or overpayment. In no event shall audits be made hereunder more frequently than once every twelve (12) months or cover any records from a period of time previously audited. The independent auditors and Licensor will be required to sign appropriate nondisclosure agreements prior to receiving any confidential information of Licensee. Licensee shall be provided with a copy of the audit report within a reasonable period of time after its completion. The cost of such audit will be borne by Licensor and not contracted on a contingent fee basis. However, in the event that the audit establishes an underpayment exceeding the greater of US$50,000 or five percent (5%) of the royalties due, Licensee shall reimburse Licensor for the cost of the audit.

3.8 Any exclusive license granted pursuant to Sections 3.3 and 3.4 shall convert to non-exclusive unless Licensee maintains a minimum aggregate royalty payment for all

Licensor-Covered Products according to the following schedule:

Calendar Year 1	US$125,000.
Subsequent calendar years when license is applicable	US$250,000.

In the event any earned royalties for Licensed Products for any calendar year (the "Earned Royalty") are less than the exclusivity-maintaining minimum royalty specified above, then Licensee may maintain such exclusivity by paying Licensor the shortfall between the Earned Royalty and exclusivity-maintaining minimum royalty specified above at the time Licensee makes the quarterly payment for the last calendar quarter for the applicable calendar year. If the Earned Royalty paid by Licensee to Licensor in any calendar year exceeds the exclusivity-maintaining minimum royalty specified above, any such excess shall be carried forward and applied to the exclusivity-maintaining minimum royalty for any subsequent calendar year.

3.9 Following the accrual of total license royalty payments from Licensee to Licensor under this Agreement of twenty-five million dollars (US$25,000,000), no royalty rate for any Licensed Product shall be above ten percent (10%) of Net Sales notwithstanding any corresponding royalty rate calculation according to Appendix C.

3.10 If Licensee fails to make royalty payments provided for in this Agreement within the time specified herein, Licensee shall pay interest on the prorated daily basis at the rate of the prevailing U.S. prime rate at that time plus two percent (2%) per year (or the maximum amount permitted by the applicable U.S. law, whichever is lower) on the unpaid balance payable from the due date until fully paid. If the amount of such charge exceeds the maximum permitted by law, such charge shall be reduced to such maximum.

3.11 All amounts due under this Agreement shall be paid to Licensor in United States currency by wire transfer to an account in a United States bank specified by Licensor or in such other form and/or manner as Licensor reasonably requests.

3.12 Licensee is not liable for any Licensor income taxes with respect to any amounts paid to Licensor by Licensee under this Agreement. To the extent any taxes are required to be withheld on royalties payable hereunder by Licensee, such taxes may be deducted and Licensee shall promptly provide Licensor with such certificates or receipts as necessary to enable Licensor to claim any applicable tax credits.

Patent Ownership of Technology Development

3.13 Employees and contractors of the Parties performing services during the Development Program shall promptly report, in a written disclosure to their respective Party, any Invention. Within fifteen (15) days after receipt, each Party shall provide to the other Party a copy of any such invention disclosure.

3.14 All patents and patent applications on Sole Invention(s) shall be owned by the Party or the Party's Affiliates whose employees or contractors made such Sole Invention(s), subject to a license granted in Sections 3.3 and 3.4 above.

3.15 Any Joint Invention, and title to all patent applications filed thereon and all patents issued thereon, shall be jointly owned by the inventing Parties. Subject to the exclusivity provisions of Section 3.3 and 3.4 and the non-compete provisions of Section 4.1, each inventing Party shall have the right to grant licenses (including the right of any licensee to grant sub-licenses) to the inventing Party's Affiliates and/or to third parties under any patent issued on such a Joint Invention without compensation to the other inventing Party and/or its Affiliates or contractors, which hereby give any necessary consent for granting such licenses as may be required by the law of any country. All expenses, other than internal legal department expenses of the inventing Parties, incurred in obtaining and maintaining such patents shall be equally shared by the inventing Parties (except as provided hereafter). Prior to filing any patent application in respect of any such Joint Invention(s), the inventing Parties shall hold consultations and agree on whether this is appropriate and, if so, which of them shall file and prosecute such application and in which countries corresponding applications shall be filed and by whom. In the event that an inventing Party elects not to seek patent protection for a Joint Invention in any particular country or not to share equally in the expense thereof with the other inventing Party, the other inventing Party shall have the right to seek or maintain such protection at its own expense in such country and shall have full control over the prosecution and maintenance thereof even though title to any patent issuing therefrom shall be joint among the inventing Parties.

7. **Term and Termination**

7.1 The initial term of the Development Program begins on the Effective Date and will continue until _____, 20XX (the "Initial Term"). This Agreement shall thereafter automatically renew without interruption for successive one (1) year periods ("Renewal Term"), unless either party gives written notice of its intent not to renew or otherwise terminate as provided in Section 7.2. For purposes of this Agreement, "Term" means the Initial Term and all Renewal Terms.

7.2 Either party shall have the right at any time, in its sole discretion, to terminate this Agreement, by giving not less than three (3) months prior written notice to the other Party of such termination. Should either Party terminate this Agreement as provided in this Section 7.2, Licensee shall be released from any obligations to make payments under Section 3.2 due or owing after such termination, but not including release from any payments due within such three-month post notification period.

7.3 Any termination of this Agreement shall result in termination of the Development Program, provided any license to Intellectual Property and any corresponding royalty obligations for Licensed Products under Sections 3.3 to 3.6 shall survive the later of ten (10) years from the Effective Date or until the last to expire of any issued patent rights included in the Licensor Intellectual Property or resulting from any Licensor Sole Invention within the Foreground Intellectual Property. To the extent the license granted in Sections 3.3 and 3.4 for a given Licensed Product does not relate to (i) any extant patent rights within the scope of Licensor Background IP or (ii) patent rights resulting from any Licensor Sole Invention within the Foreground IP, such license grant shall be deemed fully paid-up following such ten (10) year period.

7.4 If either Party otherwise fails to honor any of the material terms or conditions of the Agreement ("Breaching Party") then the other party ("Non-Breaching Party") may terminate this Agreement in a written notice enumerating the Breaching Party's breach or default(s), provided however that within thirty (30) calendar days of the date upon which the notice was sent, the Breaching Party shall be entitled to cure any of the breaches or events of default identified in the notice. If, at the end of the thirty (30) calendar day cure period, any identified breach or default has not been cured, licenses granted to the Breaching Party hereunder (including any sub-licenses to the Breaching Party's Affiliates) may be terminated by the Non-Breaching Party, effective immediately, upon written notice of termination.

7.5 Either Party's breach of the non-disclosure obligations set forth in Sections 6.1 or 6.2 shall not give the non-breaching Party the right to terminate any license, option to license, sublicense, or other Intellectual Property right granted to the breaching Party in this Agreement unless such Party has engaged in repeated and intentional breaches of such non-disclosure obligations after notice from the other Party.

7.6 Right of First Refusal

(a) If, at any time during the term of any license granted in Sections 3.3 and 3.4, Licensor or any of its controlling shareholders including Dr. Shahri Naghshineh, desire to sell part or all of the equity of Licensor (in an aggregate amount greater than ten percent (10%) of the total equity) or the assets owned by Licensor (the portion of assets or equity, as the case may be, that Licensor or any of its controlling shareholders desire to sell referred to herein as the "Licensor Business"), whether by merger, stock sale, asset sale or otherwise or in a single transaction or a series of transactions, such party or parties shall submit a written offer (the "Offer") to sell the Licensor Business to Licensee. The Offer shall disclose which assets or stock is proposed to be sold, the terms and conditions, including price and payment terms, of the proposed sale, and the prospective purchaser of the Licensor Business. The Offer shall further state that Licensee may acquire all but not less than all of the Licensor Business for the price and upon the other terms and conditions set forth therein.

(b) If Licensee wishes to purchase the Licensor Business at the price and on the terms and conditions set forth in the Offer, it shall, within thirty (30) days from the date of the Offer, notify Licensor in writing (the "Acceptance").

(c) Licensor shall not, at any time during the term of any license granted in Sections 3.3 and 3.4, in any manner convey or transfer the Licensor Business, or any part thereof, except in accordance with the terms and conditions contained in this Section 7.6.

Appendix D
Litigation Case Studies

Engage in discussions as soon as you receive patent infringement or other allegations for two reasons. First is to learn the what and why aspects, and second, to save time and position in the market place. Respond quickly and take this seriously. Here again negotiation skills come in handy, and cool heads must prevail. Settle and agree to a license. Then get on with your business. Let them worry if you are fully complying with the licensing deal, etc. In our case, the accuser refused to negotiate a licensing deal with us after we finally agreed to license their one patent. They were out to destroy our business.

These are three litigation examples my businesses were involved in.

Case A: Licensing Dispute

We licensed a small local chemical firm to make and sell our product for the domestic semiconductor fabrication market. We did not have the resources to set up our own manufacturing operations initially. The licensee had an ongoing production operation and was selling to the semiconductor fabrication niche. They had a good salesman who had been quite successful in generating domestic business for them. They were successful in securing business selling our products, but they refused to pay us the royalty based on sales as agreed upon. We found out their existing business was not making money, and they were using the revenue generated from selling our products to keep their business afloat.

We sued them and eventually settled in federal court—once our patent for the product had issued. In the meantime, we were fortunate to have set up our own in-house manufacturing operation.

Then we reached out to our product's customer in Texas and had them purchase the product directly from us. The customer mentioned they preferred purchasing the product from both sources and would continue to do so—unless we had a patent.

The following significant events are worth mentioning.

- We settled and walked away frosm $250,000 in royalties they owed us.

- Fortunately, we had only licensed this small local firm to make and sell our products in the US domestic market. We kept the rights to sell in the international market.

- Having set up our own in-house manufacturing operations allowed us to replace the licensee for the domestic accounts without any interruptions.

While we were engaged with the licensee during the first year, we had the opportunity to learn and interact with our product's end-users through the licensee to assist with sales and technology support. Interaction with the end user of your product is key as it provides essential feedback on your product's performance and improvements needed. This event was very informative in teaching us how to sell, how customers went about purchasing our products, and most important how they were using the product in their operations.

Case B: Patent Infringement

A competitor, a large publicly traded company, sent us a letter claiming one of our products' composition infringed on one of their pending patent application claims. This turned out to be incorrect as their patent claims were all initially rejected by the patent office. They also warned our existing and potential customers of the alleged patent infringement by letters sent to their respective presidents. Based on this warning, our potential customers decided against using our products and our licensee decided to terminate the license. In their initial warning letter the competitor suggested we could license their technology. Initially, we successfully defended our position in both domestic and international patent office courts, and we thought we had prevailed. However, the competitor would not give up and appealed the patent office's rejection of their patent claims in the US and South Korea. The patent office, to our total surprise and great disappointment, gave in, allowing some of the competitor's claims. Based on legal advice, we therefore decided to license their technology. However, the competitor refused! And based on our attorney's advice, we stopped promoting and selling that product of ours. This was a blow to our business. **The lesson here is: Negotiate and attempt to settle early on irrespective of your position on the alleged issue.** That is my position, but we did not, and it cost us dearly. The jury is out on whether the competitor was seriously considering licensing us in the first place or not. Based on their actions, including sending warning letters to our potential customers, I believe they had no intention of licensing us.

Fortunately for us, our licensee, a large publicly traded company, took over the negotiations with the competitor and agreed to shield us from further litigation. They settled given they must have had multiple deals with the company alleging infringement. We were not privy to the settlement deal made.

However, the licensing deal was terminated, we lost an

existing client, and a few other potential clients qualifying our product. That was unfortunate.

This is one case where licensing your product or selling the venture to a large firm can be beneficial because:

- You team up with a larger entity with more resources to market.

- They are much better positioned to defend your technology against a competitor.

- Commercialization can be expedited.

- Licensing can provide much needed revenue early on based on the agreement terms and conditions.

When you find out about another company's commercialized product infringes on your patent claims, you must notify them as such ASAP. If you knowingly ignore their product infringement on your patent, your patent may become void and unenforceable. Your approach on how to notify and contact the competitor is important and requires legal review. Your notification letter must inform the other party of the infringement and provide an opportunity for them to license your patent. Do this proactively with legal advice. Stand your ground and enforce your rights. Eventually, you should settle from a position of strength.

Case C: To Sue and Countersue Risk

If you decide to litigate for being wronged, proceed with caution. The defendant often can and will countersue. Then it is up to the lawyers, judge, and jury. Not who is in the right.

In one startup venture, the investors, including me lost money and walked away from the business. We trusted the inventor/founder because he talked a good story. I was to invest $300,000 in installments, subject to meeting certain milestones. I became the president of the venture and paid the first installment of $30,000. I started getting involved in various business activities. It took me a month to realize the founder/inventor had not disclosed all the facts about the technology limitation and the market opportunity. Soon, I resigned my position and left the business.

I know of at least four other investors who lost all their investments in the business. It is estimated more than $4 million in investments was lost. The venture ultimately closed.

I planned to sue and discussed my case with an attorney. His feedback and recommendation surprised me. He recommended I walk away. Apparently, the founder/inventor could have countersued, and I had significant exposure. The argument was the founder could claim the demise of the venture was my fault for not making the full investment! Then the outcome was up to lawyers and not the facts.

Appendix E
Founder's Agreement Overview

In my ventures, we did not have this critical agreement in place. In the first venture, we were naïve, and we made many mistakes. We were lucky the business did not implode due to conflict among the cofounders. What saved us was our board of Directors and legal counsel. They managed to keep the disgruntled cofounder from disrupting the business until the business was acquired.

In the second venture and beyond, I maintained control of the businesses by owning 100% of the voting shares and the majority of the non-voting stock.

I found this informative founder's agreement public document online from the University of Pennsylvania Law Department.

Here is an excerpt from the document.

Questions to Aid a Conversation Among Cofounders

Strategy

What goals does each of us have for the start-up?

What goals do we have for ourselves?

What are our respective timelines for these goals?

Ownership Structure

Who gets what percentage of the company?

What will we each contribute to the company? (e.g., duties, job descriptions, hour commitments, roles, and responsibilities).

How much capital are we each contributing and for what?

Is the percentage of ownership shares subject to vesting based on continued participation in the business?

Management

How are key decisions and day-to-day decisions of the business to be made? (e.g., by majority vote, unanimous vote, or certain decisions solely in the hands of the CEO).

What salaries (if any) are the founders entitled to?

How can that be modified?

What happens if one of us wants to leave?

If one founder leaves, does the company or the other founder have the right to buy back that founder's shares?

At what price?

What happens if one of us wants to sell the company, raise money, or kill the company?

What happens if one of us becomes disabled or dies?

What happens if it takes us longer than we expected to get our product up and running?

Can we each launch other startups while working on this project?

Under what circumstances can a founder be removed as an employee of the business?

What happens if one founder is not living up to expectations under the Founders' Agreement?

How would this situation be resolved?

If it turns out the business is not taking off and we decide to end our venture, can one of us take the idea and try it again?

If we need to raise start-up capital, where will it come from and how much of the company are we willing to give in exchange for that start-up capital?"

Appendix F
Exit Plan Outline

Use these prompts and answer these questions to create your own exit plan.

- Name and contact info for:
  - Exit plan advisor
  - Personal financial planner
  - Business broker
  - Accountant
  - Attorney
  - Cofounders/co-owners
  - Board of director members
  - Management team members
  - Cofounders/co-owners exit plans
  - Cofounders/co-owners role in the business exit plan
  - Owner buyout agreements
  - Talent in R&D, sales and marketing, and operations
  - Investors
- Business plan and/or prospectus
- Your market
  - What were the results of your SWOT analysis?
  - Do you have more than one market for your product?

- Your customers
  - How do you reach and sell to end users?
  - What is your sales funnel?
  - How many customers do you have in each level of your sales funnel?
  - Do you have access to multiple customers for your product/technology?
  - Does your offering save your customers time and money?
  - Does your product solve a performance issue that existing competitors' products do not?
  - What is their purchasing process cycle? (Some sales involved multiple customer departments and take up to a year or more to close.)
  - What percentage of your customers are repeat customers?
  - Do you have long-term contracts with customers?
- Your competitors:
  - Company name
  - Contact info
  - Strengths
  - Weaknesses
- Your suppliers:
  - Company name
  - Contact info
  - Strengths
  - Weaknesses
- Your backup suppliers
- Your quality control program
- Fixed costs
- Variable costs
- Net sales revenue
- Profits
- Company valuation

A Few Great Scientists I Admire

I have studied and admired these three for years. They are but a few examples of famous self-made inventors you should read up on to aid you in discovering who you are, getting to know yourself, and finding your comfort zone.

Thomas Alva Edison

American history has a special place for Edison ("one percent inspiration 99% perspiration") a self-taught scientist/chemist inventor. Edison was also brilliant at public relations and fought hard against competitors including Tesla's AC electricity system invention. Edison was well connected and a rare combination of scientist and a businessman. Edison did well in developing both disruptive and sustaining technologies. Edison formed several companies to manufacture and operate the apparatus needed for the electrical lighting system: the Edison Electric Illuminating Company of New York, the Edison Machine Works, the Edison Electric Tube Company, and the Edison Lamp Works. Edison patented a record-setting one thousand and ninety-three different inventions. He was the most prolific inventor of our times. Most of his inventions were improvements on existing products including the light bulb.

Nicola Tesla

Then there was Tesla, less known, a brilliant highly educated immigrant scientist that had no interest in finances. His electricity and electromagnetic technology inventions and their prevalence in our daily lives speak for themselves.

However, his lack of interest in business caused him to die a poor man. He struggled all his life with lack of proper financing. He had few contacts and had poor social skills. He sold his patents on AC electricity generation system to George Westinghouse for what looked like a good licensing deal. Only to give up unfortunately the royalty payments due him soon after when asked by Westinghouse. He was grateful with the initial funding he received for his patents which he promptly spent half on building a new lab to continue with his experiments. Tesla's inventions were mostly disruptive technologies that took years if not decades to be fully commercialized with the exception of the AC electricity. We are only recently paying more attention to Tesla's significant inventions and scientific contribution to advances in science and technology.

Benjamin Thompson (Count Rumford)

Finally, there was Benjamin Thompson, who is least known! Another great American scientist/engineer, inventor, spy, military officer, forward thinker and a social reformer. Thompson was well educated, connected and well travelled. He was a self-invented person with many mentors. He studied, experimented and developed like Edison many improvements over existing technologies in various industries and applications. Thompson was personable, well off thanks to marrying a wealthy widow and spent years living and working in England, France and Germany. He was always curious and in pursuit of new experiences in various sciences including in the military, nutrition and botany. He had immense glamor, a cultivated man and a great negotiator. He liked to ride, hunt and socialize. He is the inventor of drip coffeepot, the double boiler and smoke-free fireplace. Thompson inventions were for greater good. He did not establish any businesses. He was a true renaissance man.

Acknowledgments

I am grateful to my higher power for my blessings. I continue to practice the Serenity Prayer. I am not there yet.

This book is only one way of paying it forward to future entrepreneurs.

I hope to be able to continue to show my appreciation to those mentors, friends, and entities that have been supportive over the past 45 years of my ventures. I thank you and will always be grateful for those who are still with us and those who have passed on.

I must mention a few mentor's names who have passed on, who I will always remember. I am grateful for their support:

Ms. Pooran Naghshineh (my mother)

Dr. Irwin Kugelman (my graduate school advisor and boss at Lehigh University)

Mr. William Engle (Director of the city of Allentown water and wastewater division)

Mr. Lou Robinson (Manager of the first BFTP Northeastern business incubator)

Mr. James Balzano (my father-in-law and the most honest accountant and gentleman I ever met)

Mr. Fred Beste (Founder of NEPA Venture Capital and BFTP board member)

Dr. Frank Michelotti, co-owner of our first business, mentor, senior scientist, prolific inventor, and inspiration for our product's core technology in our second and third businesses.

Thank you again. I will never forget their support.

To those living mentors, I hope to be able to thank you over and over again in person.

As for you, my dear reader, you are not alone on your journey. Best wishes. May luck continue to be on your side. May you live a productive life and have fun growing and exiting your successful ventures.

I wish to inform the readers that I have decided to pursue the book objective as my full-time career. I intend to continue to learn and share with you the information I gather.

There is so much more I am learning from both the sellers and buyers of businesses. The book cannot possibly expand to contain all possible information about the M&A process. As such the reader is recommended to follow my journey at www.exitlessons.com. I am getting more significant input from buyers and sellers of businesses as I reach more contacts and do more research.

The consensus is that buyers are much more prepared than sellers and that buyers and sellers do not seem to even speak the same language and are on the opposite side of the deal . Typically, the buyer is a large publicly traded firm that uses M&A as a strategy to keep their company growing and satisfy their shareholders. The buyers purchase several smaller businesses on a regular basis. On the other hand, the sellers are often dealing with M&A for the first time in their lives. And the M&A experts/consultants (investment bankers, brokers, and lawyers) the seller retains are more interested in closing the deal than with the earn-out. These consultants typically collect their fees at closing (often paid by the buyer from the purchase price), and then they move on to their next client. They are quite busy, and their client lists are usually made up of buyers. The seller will often find most of the large investment bankers and M&A lawyers will not represent the seller due to the size of the deal being small, at less than $100 million, and due to conflicts of interest. They prefer to represent the large corporate M&A buyers. The seller is left all alone, fighting for the earn-out collection while working for the buyer or out in the cold.

There is so much more to learn and apply to our exit processes. The good news is there are many motivated startup founders and business owners out there and many more to follow. Entrepreneurs are innovators and inventors. Exits are just another obstacle we can overcome together. Good luck and best wishes.

Visit www.ExitLessons.com

You can reach me at Shahri@lbn-inc.com.

About the Author

 In August 1979, I arrived in the United States as a student from Iran, my mother country, six months after the Iranian revolution toppled the Shah Pahlavi as the autocratic king in Iran. I had been working for two years as a civil engineer for a consulting firm in Tehran Iran. My first degree is in civil engineering from Birmingham University, England.

In the spring of 1980, I started graduate studies at Lehigh University in Bethlehem, PA, as a student in the civil engineering department. I soon switched majors from civil to chemical engineering, graduating with a master's degree in chemical engineering, in 1982.

My former graduate school advisor reached out to me and offered me a research engineer position at Lehigh, which I accepted. I worked on various research projects in the environmental engineering division of the Civil/Environmental Engineering Department. While I was working there, my advisor introduced me to my future business partner.

During that time, I became increasingly disillusioned as to whether I would be content as an engineer.

So, in 1983, three of us started our first venture as a consulting firm Environmental Management Associates (EMA) Inc. A fourth cofounder join us in 1984. Based on this cofounder's experience and contacts in the rapidly growing semiconductor fabrication industry, we pivoted. We renamed our first company Advanced Chemical Technologies (ACT), Inc., in 1982. During this time, I became the president of our first venture as recommended by potential investors. We had also moved to the new Ben Franklin Technology Partnership (BFTP) of Northeastern Pennsylvania business incubator. BFTP was established as a business incubator in 1982 during Governor Richard Thornburg's term of office. The incubator supports startups with office and lab space for their research and development needs. We sold our first business in 1994. I stayed with the buyer for just under two years. Then left due insinuating circumstances and changes made in the buyer's organization.

In 1998, we started our second venture, Electronic Specialty Chemicals (ESC) , Inc. That is after I spent a few years working for a semiconductor equipment OEM firm in Allentown. I was their Vice President of Sales in Asia. The second venture was also a specialty electronics chemical firm selling to the same semiconductor fabrication industry market segment. The venture was profitable within 3 years and was purchased within five years, in August 2003. We raised the needed funds through angel investors made up of our sales reps, consultants and our lawyer. We also took out a few BFTP loans.

In our 3rd and 4th businesses, we ended up licensing our products to other larger more established firms. They were good learning experiences but not great business deals.

The following are ventures I founded, cofounded, and/ or operated as their president.

ACT, Inc.: Our first venture, ACT, Inc., took 5 years to become profitable and 10 years to be bought out. We had to learn on the job, recover from our mistakes, and pivot a few times to make it. There was significant conflict among the co-owners. We were fortunate to have sold the business before it could implode. We developed and sold specialty formulated surface preparation chemical products to the semiconductor industry. We did all our own R&D and manufacturing. We had about 35 employees.

ESC, Inc.: Our 2nd venture, ESC, Inc., took 3 years to become profitable and only 5 years to be bought out. ESC was a dream venture to own, grow, and sell. Our experienced, talented management and staff were focused, and we knew our market well. We had a great team. We raised less than $1,000,000 in equity funding from angel investors, including our independent, third-party sales reps in the United States and Europe. BFTP program provided business loans with warrants. We contracted out our production needs. We had about 30 employees.

SCD, Inc.: Initially, we were quite successful in getting traction with semiconductor fabrication industry clients. We had done business with some previously. We knew the clients well and had credibility in the industry.

However, this venture, Surface Chemistry Discoveries (SCD) closed after 3 years and assets sold. We licensed our technology to an international gas company. They initially did well in promoting and securing a major new account. SCD was unfortunately threatened with patent infringement by another large US based fortune 1000 company. This unfortunate event derailed our focus on the semiconductor fabrication industry. So, we were forced to pivot to another industry.

SurfChem Company: For our fourth business, we pivoted from the semiconductor fabrication industry to the solar cell fabrication industry. Initially, we focused on the burgeoning US solar cell fabrication industry. We were involved with 12 solar cell fabrication startup accounts evaluating our products. But almost all US-based solar cell fabrication companies shut down. The solar cell fabrication industry in US collapsed once the Chinese solar cell panels flooded the market. Attempts by us to pivot again could not be conducted in time.

LBN, Inc.: My fifth venture, self-funded, LBN, Inc., is still going, and I am still optimistic after 4 years having had to pivot a few times. For this venture we went after the Printed Circuit Board (PCB) fabrication niche in the United States.

My Other Accomplishments

- Initiating and supporting as a benefactor the set-up of the Northampton Community College (NCC) Fab Lab now part of the NCC Center for Innovation and Entrepreneurship (CIE). I sit on the advisory board for NCC CIE.

- The other visionary project was investigating and initiating the set-up of an operation now known as the City of Bethlehem, PA, Pie business incubator on the South Side.

- Initiated the set up of the Additive Manufacturing Association of Lehigh Valley (AMALV). AMALV tracks 3D printing technology advances.

I am father of three children and grandfather of two grandchildren. I enjoy hunting, fishing, astronomy, books, mentoring, and speaking at entrepreneurial events. I am available to invest, mentor, and consult with aspiring entrepreneurs.

I am now on my fifth venture. I still get inspired, excited, and motivated talking to entrepreneurs. I am inspired by innovations in many fields and by mother nature's creations. I am fascinated by human history and civilizations. I am always curious and learning.

These are exciting times for innovators given global events and the pace of technology evolutions leading to rapid changes.

Praise for Small Business Exit Lessons

"Shahri is an entrepreneur and innovator who has always been generous with his advice and perspective. His proven track record and successful business exits give credibility to his words, and I've always found his insight into our business at EcoTech helpful."

—*Pat Clasen, Founder, EcoTech*

"When I first met Shahri, our startup was at the point where we had a strong and innovative idea, but we were having trouble getting the traction we needed to reach the next level of growth. Shahri immediately recognized our potential and graciously offered his time and expertise, which were crucial in providing us the lessons we needed to start reaching our financial goals. To this day, we continue to rely on his insight and count him as one of our closest and oldest advisors."

—*Paul Hodges, Founder, Soltech*

"Shahri has the unique capability to combine a broad curiosity about technology with an intense focus on finding exploitable market niches. In his way of thinking, finding a niche is just the first step. He then sifts through the details of disruption, competition, IP, profitability, end customer motivation to change, and current vs. future market size. Only the rare niche survives that analysis, but the ones that do are gems. Shahri is tirelessly noncommittal to ideas that are partway through that analysis, sometimes to the despair of his colleagues. My advice is to listen to him."

—*Matthew D. Healy, PhD, Founder, RowChem LLC*

CPSIA information can be obtained
at www.ICGtesting.com
Printed in the USA
BVHW050016220423
662811BV00014B/1457